Blue Sky

Ed and Janice Hird

HISPUBLISHING
GROUP

www.hispubg.com
A division of HISpecialists, llc

WE DEDICATE THIS BOOK TO OUR FATHERS

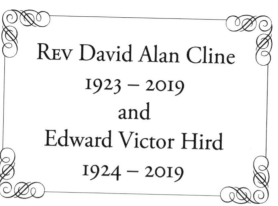

Rev David Alan Cline
1923 – 2019
and
Edward Victor Hird
1924 – 2019

As voracious readers until a few weeks
before their deaths, they both enjoyed our
Blue Sky book before they passed away at
age 95 in the Spring of 2019. They were
exemplary husbands and fathers who dearly
loved Christ and their families.

We would like to thank our good friends Bill Glasgow of Wm. Glasgow Design, Abbotsford, BC for his creative book design, Robby Grether for her Spokane-related critique, Anne Campbell for her counseling critique, Dr John Cline for his medical advice, Bob Grahame for his gifted photography, Una Stewart Cline for her great encouragement and advice, our family for all their helpful insights, and Anna Olson for her brilliant editing.

Finally we would like to thank Larry Luby, our publisher with His Publishing Group in Dallas, Texas.

Blue Sky

Published by His Publishing Group

Library of Congress Control Number: 2019914688

ISBN 978-0-9782022-5-5

eBook ISBN 978-0-9782022-6-2

Copyright © 2019, Rev. Ed and Janice Hird

First printing, 2019

HISPUBLISHING GROUP

4310 Wiley Post Rd. Suite 201
Addison, TX 75001
Ph 888.311.0811 Fax 214.856.8256

His Publishing Group is a division of Human Improvement Specialists, LLC.
For information, visit www.hispubg.com or contact publisher at info@hispubg.com

Book design by Wm. Glasgow Design, Abbotsford, BC.
Printed in Canada

Characters in the story

Sandy Brown—mother of Allie, Jerry, Josh & Charity/wife of Pastor Scott Brown

Pastor Scott Brown—father of Allie, Jerry, Josh & Charity/husband of Sandy Brown

Allie—17 years old/daughter of Sandy and Scott Brown

Jerry—15 years old/son of Sandy and Scott Brown

Josh—13 years old/son of Sandy and Scott Brown

Charity—6 years old/daughter of Sandy and Scott Brown

Vicki Broadmoor—wife of Jake Broadmoor

Jake Broadmoor—husband of Vicki, boyfriend of Rue Smith

Debra Broadmoor—mother of Jake, mother-in-law of Vicki, grandmother of Johnny and Danny

Lewis Lee—Allie's boyfriend

Rue Smith—girlfriend of Jake Broadmoor

Billy Smith—half brother of Rue Smith

Detective Cassidy—head detective, robbery section, Spokane Police Department

Detective Ewart—homicide detective, Spokane Police Department

Detective Kline—homicide detective, Spokane Police Department

Brutus—drug dealer, Tommy and Paul—his associates

Vera Brown—grandmother of Brown family

Jacob Brown—grandfather of Brown family

Sue Montgomery—friend of Allie Brown

Kerry Andrews—counselor

Janette Bingley—female District Reserve officer in the Spokane Police Department

Chapter 1

Nestled amid lovely, rounded hills dotted with Ponderosa pines, the city of Spokane, Washington, is unforgettable. The Spokane River meanders through River Park Square at the center of the city. Ponderosa pines, birches, weeping willows, and maple trees stand sentry along the hilly streets. Early in the 1900s, it was known as the healthiest city in North America. Many physical healings came through the Healing Rooms ministry, as it was called. The Brown family arrived here seven months ago in the middle of a spiritual outpouring in Spokane.

Despite the extraordinary beauty of their new city and the hope of spiritual renewal, it was hard for the Brown family to leave all their friends in Seattle. The weather was a big adjustment. For the first 25 years of their marriage, Scott and Sandy Brown had lived in Seattle's Pacific Northwest rainforest. They loved Spokane's blue sky and sunshine, all year long. However, Spokane's cold, snowy winter was daunting. Seattle, being on the Puget Sound inlet, rarely has any snow, even at Christmas time. It was good the Browns had bought a new Buick Century station wagon last year and put snow tires on it. This made them feel more secure driving in the snow and ice in the cold weather.

It was now Feb 1, 1996. The mother of the Brown family, Sandy, was very lonely in Spokane. Before she left Seattle, she had upgraded her knowledge and training in computer financial software. Her bookkeeping job at a medical clinic was a "lifesaver" but some days, there were just too many things to do at this job. Dr Morgan had decided he wanted all the patient files and financial records updated and she was having a difficult time getting it done.

Sandy was beginning to know many of her neighbors, as they went to this medical clinic. She was pondering going to full-time status, as four children were expensive! Her husband, Pastor Scott, was serving a 100-member church called Cornerstone. It was good the church owned a house that provided them with free accommodation. The church people called it a manse. But sometimes she wished they could own their own home. Though the congregation was generous, there were always extra costs with a large family. Being home after school and on weekends helped Sandy encourage her children to do their homework and get to rehearsals.

The big surprise at age 40 for Sandy was the birth of their beautiful, blue-eyed Charity. Her coloring was like her daddy. Charity was in first grade, so Sandy still needed to be home for her on weekdays after 3 p.m. Charity was always laughing and giving her family hugs. Maybe Sandy could pick up more morning hours at work, since Charity now went to school five days per week.

After picking up Charity from her school, they rushed home. The little girl needed to find her leotard for dance class, which started in thirty minutes. Just like her big sister, Allie, she was very graceful. There was a dance recital coming soon, which needed to be put on the all-encompassing kitchen calendar. As they ran in the back door to the kitchen, Sandy was surprised to find the door was unlocked. Coming through into the kitchen, she saw her son Jerry already sitting at the kitchen table, eating a beef sandwich.

Sandy asked, "Why are you home so early?" He refused to look at her and just kept eating his sandwich.

She repeated, "Jerry, why are you home already from school? Don't you have math class at this moment?"

Why won't he talk to me, what's wrong with him? Before, he would always tell me everything. Sandy thought to herself.

She stood right beside Jerry's chair, looking down at him. His shoulders were slumped and his head was down. He picked up the last half of his sandwich, turned around, still not looking at her, and left the room. Running up the stairs to his room, he slammed his door shut.

She hoped he wasn't having more trouble in math class. It worried her that he struggled in math. It was Sandy's favorite subject at college. He looked similar to Sandy with his dark brown hair and eyes. But like her daughter Allie and their dad, he struggled with math. With help from her math tutor, Allie was now doing fine in twelfth grade math. Both Allie and Jerry enjoyed music like her husband Scott, who received a degree in it before obtaining his Master of Divinity degree at Regent College. While there, he developed a lifelong fascination with strengthening marriages and family through biblical wisdom and Family Systems Theory.

The two younger children, Josh and Charity, enjoyed math and received good marks in it. Sandy would have to talk to her husband, as Jerry probably needed a math tutor, too. How they would be able to afford it, only God knew.

Running up the stairs, she pounded on Jerry's door. His door was locked and he wouldn't answer her. "Jerry, why won't you talk to me? What's wrong? Are you having trouble in math class?"

Sandy knocked again until finally, he yelled through his door, "Chill out, Mom. I don't want to talk to you right now. Don't you need to take Charity to her dance class? You better get a move on."

Sandy heard the phone ringing in her bedroom. Hurrying down the hall to her room, she picked up the phone, hoping it might be her husband. Sandy really needed to talk to him about Jerry's strange behavior.

"Is this Mrs. Sandy Brown?"

"Yes, this is Mrs. Brown. Who's this, please?"

"This is Vice Principal Stone from Whitmore High School. I'm sorry to have to tell you this. Your son Jerry has been suspended from school for skipping his math classes. I'll need you or your husband to come in and have a meeting with us here at the school before he is permitted to come back to school. It is a two-day suspension but he has already missed three days, so Jerry will have missed five days of math this week."

"This is upsetting to hear, Mr. Stone. We didn't know he was skipping his math class."

"If he doesn't attend every math class for the rest of this school year, he won't be able to continue in the music program. As you must know, music is just an elective in tenth grade and doesn't count towards graduation. Please let me know what day and time would work for you and your husband, Mr. Brown. As an extra discipline, he will also need to do a community service project."

Gripping the phone, she replied, "My husband Pastor Brown or I will phone and leave a voicemail for you today. We will let you know when we are available to come in to see you."

This news was disturbing but God had given her an inkling about his trouble with math. She'd never skipped any of her classes in high school. Her parents had expected her to do well in school. How could her son do this to her? Jerry should know better. He had always been willing to talk with her about his problems before. She felt terribly disappointed and angry with her 15-year-old son. His father was going to need to lay down the law to fix this.

Sandy phoned her husband Scott, but as usual, couldn't get through, so she had to leave a voicemail. She told him as concisely as she could about the problem with Jerry. She was so distraught her hands were shaking. Noticing the time on the clock, she ran out of the room. Calling for Charity, she quickly came down the stairs to take her to her dance class. Remembering to walk carefully, she stepped out the door onto the icy sidewalk and driveway. They jumped in the car, buckled their seatbelts and were off to dance class. The good thing was the studio was only a 15-minute drive away.

It was a lovely sunny day in Spokane, but very cold. They usually had snow and ice in Spokane for the entire month of February. Sandy needed to be careful as the roads could be slippery. They just made it to Charity's class on time.

Thank God, Sandy would still be able to get back home on time to make supper. The problem was Charity's dance teacher ignored her, even though she was obviously one of the best dancers. As she was finishing her last pirouette, Charity waved at her mom rather than looking where she was rotating. Unfortunately, this meant she turned her ankle the wrong way. Her mother watched in horror as Charity fell down and started screaming in pain. The dance instructor and her assistant hurried over. As Sandy came running to them, the teachers commented they didn't think Charity's ankle was broken. They put a frozen ice pack on Charity's ankle while she continued to whimper. They all helped the tiny, weeping blonde girl limp out to the car. Her mother didn't know if she could cope with any more bad news.

The whole family was expected for supper at 5:30. They barely made it home in time. Charity needed to have x-rays to make sure her ankle wasn't broken. Fortunately, there was a medical clinic near the dance studio. Sandy used the pay phone at the clinic to let Scott know why they might be late. Unexpectedly, there was another problem, a traffic jam on Center Street. A bus had slid into a car at a stop sign, so only one lane was open to get around the accident. She was hoping no one was seriously injured in the crash. She would check the news tomorrow to find out if there were any fatalities. It didn't look like anyone was badly hurt, from where she was stuck in traffic. She sent a quick prayer to Lord Jesus, that no one would be badly hurt and they would heal quickly. They were having leftover beef stew which Allie had just heated in the microwave. Supper was very quiet. Sandy was too troubled with Jerry to speak and couldn't eat anything. Jerry and her husband were not talking to anyone, either. Charity had hardly eaten and had gone to bed early as her ankle was aching. Her father helped her to her room after her mother gave her a pain pill. Scott was exhausted, but after supper, he took Jerry to his office. Thankfully, Josh and Allie did the dishes and cleaned the kitchen.

Scott silently walked in behind Jerry and closed the door.

"Mom told me you have been suspended from school. Tell me about missing your math classes. What's the problem?"

"Dad, there's no problem. No big deal. I don't like math, that's all."

"Really? Well, you won't graduate if you don't pass tenth grade math. Don't you want to graduate with your classmates?" His father stood by his office desk and glared at Jerry.

Jerry stood by the closed door as far away as possible from his father. He scowled right back at his father, saying loudly, "You never asked. I told you I was having trouble with math, but you ignored me."

His father looked down at the old brown carpet and felt embarrassed. "I'm sorry, son, I didn't get how much trouble you were having with it. I thought it was merely that one chapter. If you had told us, we would've found you a math tutor. Vice Principal Stone said if you don't come to every math class for the rest of this year, you will be kicked out of the music program. What'll you do then? I thought you want to be a songwriter."

His hands clenched, Jerry replied, "Dad, I can always write a song. That's what I love to do. I hate math class. I don't understand geometry. It makes me feel stupid. The kids laugh at me when I don't answer the teacher right."

Jerry continued, "I needed time to finish my song, Dad. It was hard to find any time to get it done. The only time Sammy could help me with it was during her study block. She has a great voice, and I would rather be with her than go to math class. Math is so-o-o-o boring."

Jerry's father frowned as he looked into his son's eyes. "Well, if we can get a tutor to help you understand the math, it mightn't be so boring. Okay? We'll ask Allie tonight if she can recommend a math tutor for you. There'll be a consequence, though, for you missing those classes. I will discuss with Vice Principal Stone what community service you will need to do for lying to us and skipping math class."

Jerry looked down at the old shag carpet and groaned. He abruptly sat down, sprawling on the red leather chair, and started tapping his finger on the armrest. "I didn't lie to you. I just didn't bother to tell you."

"Son, you need to tell us what's going on. Who's this Sammy? You're skipping class for a girl? No girl or song should be more important than getting through your math. Mom and I are really disappointed in you. If you'd asked, she probably could have helped you with the math. Mom's a math expert. You know how much we love you, right? I've phoned the school and made an appointment for 8 a.m. tomorrow. We will speak to Vice Principal Stone. I hope I can smooth things over for you and get you back into school for next week. In the meantime, you can do some chores around the house and shovel more snow while you are off school."

Jerry looked at him, saying in a subdued voice, "Thanks, Dad, for going with me to the meeting. I promise to go back to math. If I can get help to understand it, I can handle being in the class. I really want to be in the music program. Besides, Samantha's just a friend from the music class. It's no big deal."

Sandy was standing at the home office door trying to hear their conversation when Jerry rushed out. He bumped Sandy in the shoulder, nearly knocking her over. Without apology, he ran up to his room, slammed the door, and started playing his electric guitar very loudly.

As Scott walked out the office door, his wife put her hand on his shoulder. He was surprised to see her standing in the hall. Staring at him, Sandy asked, "Did you deal with it? Will you speak to the vice principal tomorrow? Can he go back to school?"

"Please, slow down and come into my office, Sandy. Let me tell you what we discussed privately. Jerry and I will speak to Vice Principal Stone tomorrow as I have booked an appointment. We'll let the school administrators know we will get a math tutor for Jerry. He has promised to not skip his math class anymore. I think they might suspend him for this week only. Problem solved…Let's go for a short walk around the block."

Sandy gazed thoughtfully into her husband's eyes. "Oh, Scott, don't be so sure of yourself. You can't guarantee this will solve the problem."

Giving her a hug, he took her arm and smiled at her, "You're right, dear. Sometimes I make things seem too easy." They walked out of the office, and put on their outdoor clothes, moving towards the front door. He turned to her. "Is everyone else doing their homework? Where's Allie? We need to make sure she keeps an ear out for Charity, in case she needs some help."

They walked to the living room and found Allie sitting on the couch reading a novel. There was a blazing fire in the fireplace which Scott must have made. Sandy didn't like the cold, so she hoped it would be a very short walk. She wanted to enjoy sitting in front of the fire.

Her husband called to Allie, "Mom and I are going for a short walk. Can you babysit Charity and make sure her ankle has another cold pack on it? Also, can you ask your math tutor if he can give us a name of a tutor we can hire for Jerry?"

Allie looked up from her book. "Okay, I'll listen for Charity and I'll go and help her. When Lewis Lee comes over at eight, I'll talk to him and see if he knows someone who can tutor Jerry."

Her father said, "Thanks, Allie. We'll be back in 15 minutes. Josh is in his room, hopefully working on his social studies assignment, and Jerry's in his room playing his guitar."

Once again, they started walking towards the front door. While they were walking out the door, they heard Allie in the hallway yelling at Jerry. "You're such an idiot to skip your math class."

Jerry yelled back at her. "You're the idiot. I wish I was a senior like you. It's a drag to be only in tenth grade. I don't even have a study period. My friend Sammy was only helping me write my new song during her study break. So, back off."

As they were closing the door, they heard Allie reply, "You have to go to math class or you will be in more trouble with the school. No girl is worth it. Don't do this again, Jerry."

He yelled back down the stairs, "Lay off. I already talked to Dad. He's going to talk to Vice Principal Stone tomorrow. Dad will fix everything."

As they walked down the icy sidewalk, Sandy said to her husband, "Did you hear what they said, Scott? I hope you can get Mr. Stone to agree to let him go back to school. Jerry can't afford to miss any more of his math classes. You need to find out who this Sammy girl is and warn him to not get too close to her. Remind him of our rules and our desire for him to just be her friend. He should know better and remember he's not allowed to date until age 16."

Holding each other's gloved hands, they carefully continued their walk around the block on the icy sidewalk. Scott replied to her, "Don't worry, honey. Weren't you ever a little bit wild in high school? Jerry will get his act together. I'll remind him he's not to date this girl. He wants to be a songwriter, so he has to go to his math class in order to be in the music program. He's like me, so I know he'll do it."

She stopped abruptly, let go of his hand, and stared at Scott, "But what if he doesn't get it together? As the first child, I was very responsible. Somebody has to be. My parents ordered me to obey or else I was punished. I made sure I did what they said. My sister, Hannah, was a very disobedient child and really cost my parents financially and emotionally."

Scott looked into her beautiful brown eyes and said gently, "I love you. Don't worry, dear. It's all under control. I know you were a business major, but I know how important it is for Jerry to get this song written. We have to believe in him. I'm sure Jerry will keep his word now that he has some hope in understanding math."

Sandy turned around and started trudging back through the snowy sidewalk towards home. Scott turned as well, took her gloved hand again, and walked back home, content to be with his lovely wife.

"Scott, I'm feeling nauseous. It's really upsetting to me he lied to us and pretended he was going to class when he wasn't. Jerry has missed three classes this week already, and he's suspended for two more days. Five classes he's missed. And Charity has a sprained ankle, so she won't be able to go back to her dance class for two weeks. Tomorrow she will be off school, too. I don't know if I will be able to sleep tonight with all these problems."

As they walked closely together, Scott squeezed her hand. "Sandy, everything will work out."

Coming through the front door, they took off their winter wraps and saw their daughter Allie coming towards them. Allie smiled, saying, "Good news, Mom. Lewis says he can come and tutor Jerry before he helps me tomorrow. Isn't that awesome? He will come an hour earlier Monday, Tuesday and Wednesday. Make sure Jerry's there, and Lewis will help him out. It will cost $15 per hour, the same as for my tutoring. He'll make a special exception tomorrow night and come over and tutor Jerry even though it's Thursday tomorrow. He'll explain the chapter work he has missed for this week."

Walking up the stairs to their bedroom, Sandy stopped and replied, "Thanks so much, Allie. Good night. I hope you get a good mark on your English essay tomorrow."

"It's almost done now, so I should be able to finish it. Good night, Mom and Dad. Charity already went to sleep, and Jerry and Josh are in their rooms."

Jerry was still playing his guitar when his father knocked on his door. Unlocking the door, he allowed his father to come into his messy bedroom. Jerry was relieved to hear Lewis would help him with his math tomorrow. He told his father he would make sure he got his English and History assignments done for tomorrow morning so he could drop them off. He and his father were going to be at the school in the morning at eight anyway, for the appointment with the vice principal.

Scott walked to his bedroom, looking for Sandy. She was sitting on her comfortable red-upholstered chair. Standing in front of her, he told her about his conversation with Jerry.

He prayed, "Lord Jesus, I thank you Charity didn't break her ankle. We pray Jerry will be able to go back to school next week. I pray God, you give my wife Sandy, who has had all this trauma today, the peace that passes understanding. Lord, I pray as Jesus says that tomorrow will worry about itself, rather than Sandy having to do it. We pray for the victims in the car/bus accident that they will quickly heal. Lord Jesus, would you give Sandy a good night's sleep? Thank you, Jesus. In your name. Amen"

Sandy replied, "Thanks so much for the prayer. This is good news for Jerry. I hope I can sleep soon."

It was only ten, so Scott went back downstairs to his office. Being a night owl, he liked to stay up late and get up late. With Sandy, ten was her limit as she liked to be awake at six every morning. She got undressed and put on her pajamas, reaching for her most recent Jane Austen novel. She was really enjoying Sense and Sensibility. Turning on the bedside lamp, falling into bed, and pulling up the covers, she finally relaxed. Sandy looked forward to losing herself in the story. But she had trouble concentrating on the words and kept reading the same page over and over again. Finally, she put the book away and remembered again all that had happened through the day. She was saddened her lovely little Charity had hurt herself. She prayed her daughter would receive a miraculous healing. She also prayed the people in the car/bus accident would be okay. Finally, she asked God that Jerry would go back to being the good student he had always been, including succeeding in math. She concluded with protection prayers for the whole family.

Jerry's behavior was a very discouraging memory from the day. She now understood why he wouldn't talk to her. He must have been embarrassed to have been caught skipping his math class. Her husband privately believed that Jerry would soon have a hit song in the music industry but Sandy was not convinced. Scott had tried to persuade her this could be true. There was no point in disagreeing, as he would try to push his viewpoint. She didn't want to have any more quarrelling with him. She was feeling exhausted after the very busy day at work, Charity's sprained ankle, the traffic accident, and Jerry's problems with school.

While she lay there desperately trying to sleep, Scott came in the room, got undressed, and got into his side of the bed. He turned over, gave her a kiss and said good night. Turning off his bedside lamp, he immediately went to sleep. How unfair! She wished she could go to sleep quickly like him.

Chapter 2

Two weeks later, Jerry was all smiles as he rushed in the kitchen door right before dinner. The family was sitting down at the table. Sandy hoped Jerry had good news about math class.

Jerry laughed, saying, "I've been going to math class all week and it's starting to make sense to me. Lewis Lee is a great tutor. Thanks for your suggestion for a tutor, Allie. I got 63 percent on my last quiz. I'm so happy. Guess what else?"

Turning to him, both Charity and Allie asked, "What, Jerry?"

"I got an A for the song I wrote. Samantha accompanied me on the piano. It's called 'Peace for You'. The music teacher agreed I can make a demo in the music studio," he replied as he passed the potatoes to his father.

His father said, "Wow, I'm glad you passed your math quiz and thrilled you got such a good mark on your song. Congratulations. Isn't this great, everybody? Now let's say grace."

The whole family nodded their heads, "Yes." They bowed their heads as their father prayed, "For what we are about to receive, may the Lord make us truly thankful. In Jesus' name. Amen."

Their father asked, "Who'd like to hear Jerry's song?"

Sitting at the kitchen table, everyone nodded their heads again, looking eagerly at Jerry. Josh, who was sitting beside Jerry, bumped him on the shoulder. "Right, when can we hear it, bro?"

"I don't know. I think it sounds better on the tape recording, but I guess I could just play it for you on my guitar," answered Jerry as he chewed on a piece of steak.

"But Jerry, don't you have math homework you need to finish tonight?" asked his father.

"Yeah, I do, Dad, but Lewis is coming over at seven to help me with math. I also have history and English homework, but if I do it now, I can play it for you on my guitar." He finished eating the food on his plate, and rinsed his dinner plate in the sink. Running up to his bedroom, he brought down his guitar, and sang the song for them. Everyone congratulated him on the great tune.

Scott smiled at his wife and said, "What a wonderful song, Sandy! It's just like we hoped. And Jerry will be able to finish tenth grade."

"I sure hope this happens. I pray he will pass all his courses, especially math."

Sitting beside Sandy, he whispered under his breath, "Please don't worry about him. It's not good for your blood pressure. God will make a way."

Charity, listening intently, said, "What's wrong with Jerry? Is he sick?"

Her father replied, "No, honey, he's just having trouble with math."

Charity replied, "My ankle's fine now because you prayed for it, Daddy. What about praying for Jerry, so he can do well in math? Maybe I could help him. I know how to count to 100 now."

Everyone chuckled, except Charity, who looked puzzled.

Her father said, "Charity, Jerry knows how to count to 100. It's tenth grade geometry he's having trouble doing. But thanks for offering to help him."

"Oh," Charity replied and smiled. She got out of her chair and ran to the living room to watch cartoons. Everyone was relieved to see her ankle was all healed.

Josh looked at his dad and piped up, "I'm good at geometry, so maybe I could help him, Dad."

His father replied: "Well, if it was eighth grade geometry, I'm sure you could help, but these are tenth grade proofs. Thanks for offering, Josh. Okay, since Jerry's gone to get ready for his tutor, Josh, let's finish clearing the table and putting the food away in the fridge. Sandy, I'll finish putting the dishes in the dish washer. I'll ask Allie to wash the pots and pans. Josh, go tell your sister I need to speak to her, please."

"Sure, Dad."

Scott turned to Sandy and said, "Dear, why don't you take a break? You deserve it. This was a great dinner. Oh, I need to remember to talk to Jerry about the community project we have found for him to do. See you later."

After finding Allie, Josh put the leftover food away in the fridge. Allie proceeded to wash the pans, while her father finished putting the dishes in the dish washer. The phone rang in the kitchen. Josh answered it. At thirteen, he always hoped it would be for him, but usually, it was not the case

He ran to the hallway and reached his mother before she started up the stairs to her bedroom.

"Mom, phone call for you. It's Mrs. Broadmoor."

Sandy took the handset from Josh and said, "Hi, Vicki. How're you?"

Vicki Broadmoor replied, "I'm not good. Can you come over and talk with me? Things are bad."

"Sure, Vicki. I think that'll work. Just let me check with Scott. I need to make sure he doesn't have a meeting tonight, so he can put Charity to bed."

After checking with Scott and getting his agreement, she drove over to Vicki's house. It was a bright, cold night but the roads had been cleared. She noticed the blue two-story house looked fine except none of the sidewalks had been cleared and the driveway was full of snow. Sandy parked on the icy street. When Vicki opened her front door, she whispered that her children were already in bed for the night.

Sandy was shocked to see how run-down Vicki appeared. Her long brown hair was lanky and unwashed, and her bloodshot green eyes had dark circles under them. She looked exhausted. Vicki appeared to have lost ten pounds in the last two weeks.

Sandy came in the door, hung her coat and hat in the front closet and turned to Vicki. Closing the door, Vicki locked it and bolted it as well. She gestured to Sandy that they should go into the living room. Sandy sat down on the couch.

"Vicki. Come sit down with me and tell me what's happening."

"I don't know how I can tell you." Vicki started weeping profusely as tears flowed like a river down her face. Sandy started praying under her breath.

After five minutes of Vicki's tears, Sandy turned to her and said, "Can you please tell me what's going on? Where's Jake? I don't see his car."

As she continued to weep, Vicki said between sobs in a quiet little voice, "That's the problem. Jake isn't here. He left me for another woman at his office. I'm stuck here because two weeks ago, he moved out and took our Chevrolet Caprice. You know how difficult it is to get around the city with two little boys and no car."

Vicki looked down at her feet. Sandy moved over, putting her hand on Vicki's arm. She felt sad for her, and very angry at Jake.

Vicki continued, "I don't know how to tell his mother Debra. She has been phoning me to say she would like to come over and see the boys, but I have been putting her off. I haven't had the nerve to tell her what's happened. Jake is her only son who she loves very much. I don't want to hurt her. This may destroy Debra."

Sandy looked down, replying quietly, "Oh, honey, I'm so sorry. Can I give you a hug? Will you let me tell Scott about this so he can pray for you? He might have some good advice for you." Vicki nodded her head. Sandy moved closer, giving her a huge hug while Vicki continued crying.

"I don't know, Sandy. I feel so ashamed he has left me. Maybe Pastor Scott could help. Jake hasn't given me any money since he left. I'm running out of cash as he has control of our bank account. The money automatically goes into his bank account because he is the financial expert." Vicki looked down at her slippers.

"Well, Vicki, if Jake stays with this woman and doesn't come back, make sure you receive child support. Do you have a lawyer? Pastor Scott can help you with this."

"No, I don't have a lawyer. I want Jake to come back. I don't want to divorce him. He's my husband. I'm praying and believing God will bring Jake back to me. The boys and I need him." She started weeping loudly again. Sandy patted her on the back, continuing to pray silently.

After a while, Vicki spoke again while looking out the window. "We've been married for ten years. I miss him so much. How could he do this to me? Jake hasn't returned any of my phone calls over the past two weeks. I don't know what to do."

"Will you let me pray for you, Vicki? Do you have time tomorrow? I could phone Pastor Scott now and see if he has time tomorrow afternoon? He could let you know if you need to speak to a lawyer. What do you think? Also, we have food vouchers, or I could give you some food if you need some."

Vicki lifted her head and nodded as Sandy looked her in the face, giving her an encouraging smile.

"I guess you could pray for me. We have enough food at the moment. I don't have a lawyer or a babysitter. The only one who looks after the children is my mother-in-law, Debra. But I didn't want to upset her by dragging her into this mess. Okay, I'll talk to Pastor Scott. I have time in the afternoon. But who will babysit my boys? I can't ask my mother-in-law."

"Well, Vicki, tomorrow I have the day off from work, so I could babysit for you. If I phone Scott, we could see when he has time to meet you, at the church office. If you can finish by 2:30 p.m., I can get Charity from school."

Sandy walked with Vicki into the kitchen. Instinctively reaching for the phone with her left hand, she dialed their number. Scott answered the call on the third ring.

She said to him, "Scott, this is very confidential. Do you have time to see Vicki Broadmoor tomorrow at one, in your church office? Remember, if this works for you timewise, I need Vicki to be back here at her house at 2:30, so I can still drive Charity from school."

He replied, "Let me check my planner."

Scott looked at his daily calendar sitting on his desk, picked up the phone and said, "Okay, Sandy, that time will work tomorrow. Please let Vicki know. Are you going to babysit her children for her?"

Glancing at Vicki, she smiled and said, "Yes, I can babysit for Vicki."

Vicki appeared relieved. Sandy gave her another hug, saying she would see her tomorrow at 12:45, and Pastor Scott was expecting her at one at the church office. Sandy was happy to drive the ten blocks home and go back to her own loving family.

Chapter 3

S andy arrived at Vicki's place right after lunch the next day. It was another chilly "blue sky" day in Spokane. She gingerly walked onto the icy walk towards Vicki's door. Opening the front door, Vicki started walking carefully down her front sidewalk to meet her. It was actually good Vicki's sidewalk hadn't yet been cleared. There was a surface for their boots to walk on. Maybe when it melted a bit, Sandy could get Josh to come over to Vicki's in order to clear the ice and snow off the sidewalks.

Vicki whispered to Sandy, "Johnny and Danny are both asleep. The front door is unlocked, so help yourself to a hot drink in the kitchen. There's boiling water in the kettle, if you want some tea. Hot coffee is in the carafe. The boys had a busy morning playing and running in the gym at the recreation center so they were tired out."

She continued with some animation in her face, "We went to the new moms' group. Some of the others in the group are single moms, so they understand the pain I am going through and encouraged me to go and see your husband for advice. I'll be back by 2:30. It's a good thing I have sturdy snow boots as it takes a while to walk over to Cornerstone Church. I've left a bottle in the fridge in case baby Johnny is hungry when he wakes. Just warm it by setting it in hot water in a large bowl."

"Yes, Vicki. I'll do that. Also, I'll give Danny a drink of milk in his sippy cup if he wakes as well. Be careful walking over there. I'll see you later."

Scott was deeply concerned for Vicki and her children. He was grieved to hear from Sandy that Jake had left Vicki without even attempting marriage counseling. When Vicki arrived at the church, Pastor Scott was shocked to see how much Vicki had changed. It had only been a few weeks since she had been to church. Her face was pale and blotchy from crying. In the past, she had always had a pleasant smile on her face. Now she would not even look at him. Her big, green eyes were filled with tears and she didn't say a word. Her back was bent, and she looked exhausted.

"Vicki, please come in and have a seat. Can I give you a tissue?" Pastor Scott said as he stood in front of his desk chair. He gestured to a comfortable brown fabric chair, across from his desk. This would make it possible for him to see and talk to her easily.

Vicki nodded, sat on the chair and took the Kleenex box. After several moments, she mumbled, "I told Sandy she could tell you what had happened when she returned home last night. Did she tell you my husband Jake has left me? He wouldn't even discuss it with me. The day he came home from the computer conference in Seattle, he went to our bedroom and started packing his suitcase. When I asked him what he was doing, he said he had found someone else he was moving in with. I pleaded with him to not do this, asking him what I'd done wrong. At first, he wouldn't even talk to me. He just continued packing his clothes."

Pastor Scott replied, "Did Jake say anything else to you as he was leaving that night?"

Vicki responded, "When he was running down the stairs, he stopped for a moment, stared back at me, saying this new woman makes him feel young and carefree. He complained I only talk about being in debt or when I need him to help me with the boys. Jake claimed I'm always nagging him and I'm no longer any fun. He asked me why he always has to be the one to get up in the middle of the night when one of the boys is sick. Didn't I know because Jake's the only one with a 'real job', he needs his sleep? He also complained I never dress up for him anymore, or make an effort when he wants to sleep with me. But I told him it was because I'm always so tired from breast-feeding the baby."

"I'm saddened to hear this, Vicki," Pastor Scott replied as he looked down at his desk.

Vicki continued, "Pastor, sometimes I feel like giving up. Our three-year-old Danny runs around the house making messes all day long. I feel exhausted from constantly trying to keep the house clean the way Jake likes it. When I told him how weary I was, he shrugged his shoulders, ran down the last two stairs and slammed the front door. How can he blame me when I'm trying so hard?"

Vicki started to cry again. Pastor Scott gave her a tissue and started praying silently. He looked her in the eye and said, "Do his close relatives know he's done this to you, Vicki? Maybe they could talk some sense into him. How long has he been gone now? One week, is it?"

She shook her head, replying, "He's been gone now for exactly two weeks. His mom and sisters don't know he's left me. They've been phoning me and asking where he is, as they haven't heard from him either for the last two weeks. I haven't had the nerve to return their phone calls or voicemails."

As Vicki glanced at him, she continued, "He left me for a 24-year-old woman named Rue Smith, who's the new computer expert at his office. I phoned Laura who works for Jake, but still doesn't know he's left me. She said he's been looking very tired lately. The secretary commented the young men in the office are attracted to Rue Smith, as she wears very short skirts and tight blouses, and flirts with all of them. I don't know why she wants my husband when there are lots of younger men who are interested in her. But as the boss, he makes the most money, and has control over promotions and raises."

She turned her head, looked out the window, and said, "He told me he was going to be living at Rue Smith's loft. I can't believe he would betray me. It makes me want to puke. My little boys really miss their daddy. I don't understand why he hasn't even tried to see his children, even if he doesn't want to see me. Doesn't he get it? They're little and they need their daddy. Danny, at three, cries himself to sleep at night, asking Jesus where his daddy is."

Pastor Scott looked down at Vicki's bowed head. Hopefully, he could reach Jake and get him to change his mind.

He replied, "This is horrible. Do you think Jake might be willing to talk to me? Perhaps Debra could get him to phone me. Do you want me to recommend a lawyer for you? I know several who could advise you on how you can get Jake to give you child support."

He went over to his file cabinet and started looking through his rolodex.

"Vicki, I will make some calls today and find an attorney who can help you pro bono. We need to ensure you and your sons are protected."

"Yes, please, but I don't want a divorce," said Vicki. "Without his support, I'm so exhausted, so lonely, so miserable. Jake was such a kind man when I first knew him. It doesn't make any sense. I pray Rue Smith soon finds another man. How dare she take my husband? I'm so angry at her I feel like spitting."

He responded, "This is really tough for you, Vicki. We will be there for you. I'll do some research on attorneys, and put you in touch with a good one. This doesn't mean I think you should get a divorce. We hope your marriage will get back on track. However, this will take time and prayer. But in the meantime, we need to get Jake to give you access to the bank account. Is it alright if I speak to your mother-in-law Debra about getting Jake to give you bank access?"

"No, Pastor. I will speak to Debra myself about financial access. Thank you so much for your time."

"Jake needs to give you child support. Let me know when you want to talk again. In Family Systems Theory they encourage you to stand on your own two feet. Don't let Jake's bad behavior take you out. Your mother-in-law Debra deserves to know what's happening with Jake. She probably already knows something in her spirit, as she's a mighty prayer warrior."

"I need to walk home now so Sandy can pick up Charity at school. Thanks again for seeing me on such short notice. I guess I'll be brave and call my mother-in-law. Bye."

Ten minutes later, Vicki opened the door of her house. Sandy said, "Hi Vicki, how did it go? Were the sidewalks clear? I hope Scott helped you."

Vicki said quietly as she closed the door, "Yes, the sidewalks have been cleared. It was good to get out in the sun. Pastor Scott is going to phone some lawyers and find the right one to help me. I'm glad about this. I'm also happy I was able to get back in time for you to pick Charity up from school."

Sandy turned. "Thanks. I will phone you later tonight or tomorrow, and see how things are going. Your boys are still sleeping. If you need some money the church has a fund to help people in difficult situations."

"No, Sandy, I will check with Debra first and ask her what she thinks. With your encouragement I'm feeling better. I'm hoping she'll help us out temporarily with our finances."

Vicki waved at her as Sandy got in her car. A few minutes later, she sat at the kitchen counter and prepared to call her mother-in-law. It was hard for her to do this. Debra was great but Vicki really missed her own parents who had died in a car crash five years ago. She took a large breath, exhaled, and dialed Debra's phone number.

"Hello Debra, this is Vicki."

Debra replied in a relieved tone, "Hello dear. Where've you been? I haven't been able to reach you for a few weeks. I leave you messages but you haven't returned my phone calls. I even dropped by the house several times but you were never there."

Vicki screwed up her courage, said a prayer under her breath and said, "I hate to tell you this, Debra, but Jake has left me for another woman. Because I've been so depressed about it, I haven't let you know. He's been gone for two weeks now. The boys and I are so distressed by this. We miss him very much."

"Vicki, I'm so sorry. What's wrong with him? Why didn't you call me? I would have come over and helped you with the boys. I did reach Jake at the office last week, but he said he was too busy to talk. When I told Jake that I would like to come over to your house for a visit, he said I needed to talk to you about that. Now I know why."

"I was wrong to hide this from you. I didn't want to upset you. I would like you to come over, Debra. I hate to ask but I don't have any cash to buy food. Jake has always controlled the money. My phone calls to him just go to voicemail. The only good thing is I have a big freezer and have lots of dried goods in the cupboards," Vicki said quietly.

Debra replied, "This is terrible. What's wrong with my son? I'll find out what's going on. I'll help you out with some money today until we can get Jake to take care of you and the boys. Would you like me to take you food shopping now?"

"Oh, thanks so much. You're a life saver. It would be great to get some fresh vegetables and fruit. The boys don't eat much of those, but I've been missing fresh vegetables. Can you come over soon? The boys are just waking from their naps. They'd be happy to see you. I've been going to a group at the recreation center to have someone to talk with about this. The boys enjoy being there at the rec center, since it's too cold to play outside in our backyard. We've been visiting the rec center every day to get a break from the cold weather. I think that's why you haven't been able to find me at home. It's wonderful it's nearby so we can walk there. I can pull both of them on our sled."

"I'll be over in 20 minutes. I'm so looking forward to seeing Danny and Johnny. They're such sweet little boys."

"Oh great, thank you, Debra. We're really looking forward to seeing you, too. Sorry for not telling you this bad news sooner. It'll be wonderful to see you again."

"Since you can't get any money from Jake, I'll go to his office and make sure to get some from him. I'm dismayed to hear he has treated you like this. You don't deserve this. You've been good to him and my grandsons. I'll pray he will come to his senses. See you soon."

Vicki was relieved to hear Debra speak kindly to her. She sat down and had a little cry, before taking a deep breath and calming down. She wished she had told her mother-in-law sooner but finally she had a reason to smile for the first time in two weeks.

Chapter 4

Being a musician, Jerry had found it hard to move away from all his friends in Seattle just before he started tenth grade. It was a huge letdown for him to go to a small city like Spokane when he was used to the large metropolis of Seattle. Instead of being a popular sophomore at his Seattle high school, he had to begin all over again, trying to make new friends in this unfamiliar city. Being in the music class at Whitmore High School had proven a great way to make friends. It had a first-rate music program with a songwriting component, as well.

Jerry had some great pals now at his new school, including Samantha. She was not only super talented as a song writer and musician, but was also hot. She had huge blue eyes and long blue-black hair. Samantha was tall and slender like Jerry, though he was a little taller at six feet. Sometimes he had to be careful with her. She had a quick temper. He didn't like to hide things from his parents but they wouldn't approve. They didn't know how appealing Samantha could be when she would cozy up beside Jerry at his locker. He lived for her hugs.

His father and his mother had always encouraged him to honor girls. They didn't want him to date yet, even though he was 15. Most of the boys in tenth grade already had steady girlfriends. Jerry wanted to have a girlfriend like everybody else. He considered Samantha his girlfriend and so did she.

It was Monday, with music class right after lunch. Jerry waited eagerly for lunch hour to be over so he could go to music class and see Samantha. She had a different schedule than his since he was in arts and she was a science major. This meant Jerry could only eat lunch with her on half-day Wednesdays.

As Jerry sauntered into the music room, his friend Jim tapped him on the shoulder and said, "What's up, Jer? How's the new song going?"

"It's all good. How about you, Jim? Does Mr. Rush like your song?" Jerry tapped Jim's shoulder back and smiled.

Jim shook his head and shrugged his shoulders. "I don't know. I'm still waiting to find out what grade they gave me for my song. I'm trying to stay chill about it. Have you seen Samantha lately?"

Jerry stared at Jim. "What's it to you? We haven't seen each other since last Friday as she had the science fair on the weekend. Besides, I was busy working on improving my song."

Jim smirked as he hit Jerry on the arm. "Well, I saw her with Rick Chambers on Saturday night at the movies and they were sitting close together. She was all over him." He smirked again and watched to see what Jerry would do with this news.

Jerry stared at Jim, stood beside him and spoke into his ear, "Don't go there. I'm sure it was just a group thing. I'll ask her when I see her today in class."

Jim turned around, leaned into Jerry and whispered back in to his ear, "Jerry, I didn't see anyone else near them. I was sitting with Jody, Cliff and Shane, and we all saw them. You better find out what's happening."

Jerry pushed Jim away from him and said, "Shut up. I can't talk now. Here she comes with Kathy and Lyle."

As Jerry watched Samantha stroll into the music room, she looked towards him, waving at Jerry. He smiled at her and walked right up to her. "Hey, beautiful. Where did you get that gorgeous red sweater?"

Samantha edged right beside Jerry, touched him with her arm and replied, "How's my favorite guitar player? I got it at the Gap. It's great, isn't it? Is that a new jean jacket? Jerry, you look really cool. I hope you got your song done so we can record it today."

She laughed and continued speaking while still rubbing against him with her arm. "Guess what? I won first prize for my computerized rocket project at the science competition on the weekend. Isn't that cool? Rick Chambers was my partner. We celebrated with our friends by going to *Apollo 13* on Saturday night."

Jerry replied, looking at her carefully, while she still was touching him on the arm, "Yeah, Jim was telling me he saw you there with Rick having a real good time."

Samantha looked down and abruptly took her hand off Jerry's arm. "Julie and Sean from my science lab were with us as well, so he's wrong. They must've been out in the lobby buying popcorn or something, because they sat with us for the whole movie. It wasn't a date, just a celebration for winning. Just chill, Jerry."

Jerry frowned and pulled away, but Samantha turned around to give him a big hug from behind. She abruptly let go when she saw their teacher, Mr. Rush, coming into the music room.

Samantha punched Jerry lightly on the shoulder and whispered in his ear, "You're the only one for me, Jerry, so don't be shy because you're still my guy." And she giggled.

Jerry looked back at her and smiled. Samantha ran over to check with Mr. Rush about recording Jerry's song. He agreed they could use the recording studio for the entire class time. Samantha and Jerry linked arms as they walked with into the recording studio together, firmly closing the door. She put on her earphones and began playing Jerry's song on the synthesizer. He strapped on his red Gibson guitar, put on his earphones, and started strumming the rhythm section of the song into the instrument microphone. An hour later, they had finished the first track of his song. They agreed the next time they had music class, they would lay down the vocal tracks for his song "Peace for You." He loved singing and playing music with her. It was such a rush to be with her.

Jerry looked at his watch. "Samantha, I've gotta go to math. I'll miss being with you, but I can't skip any more classes, or they'll kick me out of the music program. So, we'll need to work on this song outside of class. Can you make any time after school this week?"

Samantha smiled brightly, "Give me your number. I'll call you after supper tonight. I have dance class right now, so I've gotta run."

Jerry gave her a big grin and said, "Okay, here it is. Talk to you later."

At seven that evening, the phone rang in the Brown house. Josh answered the phone, looked surprised, covered the mouth piece and muttered, "Jerry, you have a phone call. It's a girl."

Jerry turned red and quickly ran to the wall phone, taking the handset from his brother. He was relieved no one else was in the kitchen.

"Hey, Jerry, this is Sammy. I don't have time to work on your song after school this week. We'll just have to try and get it done during music class. Okay? Maybe we can work on it after school in the music room next week, instead?"

"Oh, next week would work too. Cool, I will talk to you at school. See ya," he replied.

Josh was still in the kitchen, because he was so slow putting the dishes in the dishwasher when it was his turn.

"Who was that, Jerry?" Josh said as he stood beside his brother and put his arm around him.

Jerry pushed him away, stared at him and replied, "Oh, she's just a girl I know in my music class. She's helping me with my song. Don't tell Mom and Dad that she phoned, please?"

Josh looked back at him. "Well, why can't I tell them? What's the big secret? Is she an alien or something?"

"Of course, she's not an alien, you dope. No big secret. I'm not really dating her, at least not officially. But we have an understanding."

"Okay, big brother, I won't tell them some girl phoned you. Besides you haven't told me her name, so how can I tell the parents?" Josh replied, giving Jerry a wink.

Chapter 5

A month ago, Jake had found it thrilling to meet Rue Smith. She was a tall, blue-eyed, long-haired blonde with an alluring figure. Rue had applied for and won the job of computer financial expert at his office, thanks to her excellent referrals and resumé. She was not only beautiful, but fun to work with. She was very clever and knowledgeable with computers. Rue had turned out to be a huge asset to the office.

Two weeks ago, Jake had requested Rue come with him to a Seattle conference on financial planning. He was glad they had travelled by air, since driving in the winter to Seattle would take a minimum of five hours on the snowy roads. Also, he was afraid to drive through the mountains in the winter as his wife's parents had both died five years ago in a car accident while driving through a winter storm in the Washington mountains. The passes could be extremely hazardous in the deep snow. There were fatal accidents every winter. February could be especially dangerous, being prone to avalanches or fog. Jake didn't need that hassle.

The computer conference was at the huge Sheraton Hotel in Seattle, Washington. He couldn't believe it. A beautiful woman like Rue wanted to sit beside him at the conference. Many other men there were vying for her attention. He had always been faithful to his wife, so he didn't know why Rue made him feel so excited and interested in her.

It was unusual for Jake to leave his family at home. However, this particular time he didn't have the money or time to bring his family with him. His loud and energetic little boys made it hard to concentrate and study at night while he tried to prep for the next day at the conference. It was tough making it financially at the moment with his business, Broadmoor Financial Services, Inc. It had been so much better when he still had his partner, Jonathan Westly, doing the computer part of the business. He was really missing Jonathan.

Jake hoped Rue could be as reliable as Jonathan had been. Rue was such a flirt it was sometimes hard to get any work done. It made him happy to be sitting with her at the conference. She had a great bubbly personality and all the men sitting near her laughed at her jokes. His wife Vicki used to be funny when they first dated. Now Vicki just seemed to complain all the time about his busyness and the lack of money.

After dinner, Rue was sitting at the Tahiti Bar on the ground floor of the Sheraton. A sizable group of young men from the conference surrounded her. When Rue saw Jake come into the bar, she called him over and said she had been hoping he would come by for a drink. Leaving her bar stool and admirers, Rue took her wine glass and sat at a private corner table with Jake. Without asking, she ordered a screwdriver for him. He drank it quickly, as he didn't want to look unsophisticated. The drink gave him quite a buzz. He'd never drunk hard liquor before.

"Jake, tell me about yourself." Rue looked into his face and smiled at him.

Jake glanced at her and then away. "Not much to tell. I have a wife I love very much and two wonderful little boys. I went to North West Community College and got a degree in finance. Three years ago, Jonathan and I started this financial planning business. He left six weeks ago to start his own company in Seattle. He's an expert with computers so we really miss him. That's why we've brought you on board."

Rue continued to edge closer to Jake, eventually sitting right beside him at the table. "From what I have seen so far, it looks like the company's financial records are in great shape. You and Jonathan have done an amazing job, Jake."

Rue waved to the waiter and said to Jake, "Do you want another drink?"

Jake shook his head no, moved away from her and said, "No thanks, Rue. I need to go to my room and phone my wife."

Just as he was leaving, Rue put her hand on top of Jake's hand. "We really need to sit and talk more about work. It won't take long. You can phone your wife later."

With her gorgeous eyes, she gazed intently at him. Moving to sit right beside him again, she started rubbing his leg with her shoe. Jake found this very provocative. He moved closer to her and responded, "I really need to go and phone Vicki. But maybe we can discuss work for a little bit." Jake looked at his watch. "Besides, it's probably too late to phone my wife now, anyway. It's nine. I can phone her in the morning when the boys are awake, too."

With her strong encouragement, he took another drink of the second screwdriver she had ordered for him. As he looked away for a moment and thought about Vicki, Rue dropped some powder into his drink. Jake didn't notice this. He wasn't used to drinking hard liquor, so he didn't notice the funny taste. Rue smiled to herself. She was very pleased he'd finished the second drink. He started sliding out of his chair. Before he fell on the floor, Rue grabbed him. Putting his arm around her, she helped him out the door of the bar.

When he opened his eyes the next morning, he was shocked to find he was lying in Rue's bed in her hotel room. He didn't remember getting there, but here he was beside her. She gazed at him and motioned for him to come closer.

"Wow, that was a great night we had. You were amazing," she murmured and looked over at him again.

Jake looked back at her, noticed she didn't have clothes on and said, "I don't recall what happened last night. I can't remember anything. How did I get here?"

Rue smiled, "You walked here, of course, silly. Let me remind you what happened last night. Why don't we try it again, right now?"

Two weeks later, Jake still couldn't remember how he had got so involved with Rue. He was starting to wonder how Vicki was doing, and really missed his little boys. Why did he leave his wife? As Vicki had left him several messages, Jake thought to himself that maybe he should respond back. However, he didn't know what to say, since he had a new life now.

Jake hadn't liked Vicki nagging him. Nobody had the right to tell him what to do with his life. Whenever he thought about phoning his family, he assumed Vicki would be angry and yell at him so he didn't call.

Besides, Rue would be right there asking him something about work or taking him out to another bar every day after work. She seemed to always be close by when he thought about phoning Vicki. Rue never made dinner, instead they constantly went out to restaurants. She seemed to live on yogurt and fruit. Every day for breakfast, it was the same thing. Jake was getting tired of it.

Jake decided Rue was a workaholic. She was at the office till eight or nine. He had to be there as well, since the files were confidential, and she didn't have access unless he was there in the room with her. Just as he was going to leave for the day at seven, Rue came into his office.

"Where're you going? You can't leave yet. We need to look at the Creston Account. There seems to be an irregularity with the cash flow in their mining portfolio."

Taking the file, Jake said, "Let me see it. Where? It looks fine to me. I'm exhausted. I don't want to stay late tonight. I need to phone my mother Debra and see how she's doing."

"Your mother's fine. Get a grip. We need to work on this before tomorrow so they don't think you're cooking the books, Jake. I'm here working overtime tonight to protect you."

"What're you talking about? I've never done anything illegal in my life. I'll get the office files audited tomorrow, if you think there is a discrepancy."

"Jake, you look stressed. Okay, it's probably nothing. We can look at the file tomorrow morning. Let's go back to my loft and have a good time."

"Sorry, I need to go and see my mother. She keeps phoning me. I need to make sure she's okay."

"Jake, don't be ridiculous. Come with me now." Rue came towards him and tried to give him a hug. But Jake pushed her away and walked out to the reception area. She followed him out, swore at him and said he'd regret it if he didn't come with her immediately.

He turned to her and said, "No one has the right to tell me what to do. I'm allowed to see my mother and my family. How dare you try to stop me? I'm sick and tired of drinking coffee bought in a coffee shop and eating canned food. That coffee you give me tastes vile. I'm not drinking it anymore. I want to see my wife and my sons."

Rue scowled at him. "Jake, if you do that, don't bother coming to my place again. You'll not be welcome. Two weeks ago, you left your wife and you haven't missed her. What's with you tonight? Your wife is boring and overweight, and you know it. Let's go have fun at my place. Remember, I'm the one who knows how to please you. Come on." And she reached out her hand to him.

Jake stared at her for a moment, before rushing out of the office, slamming the office door. He started driving over to his mother's. Rue wondered what had happened to him. Hadn't he drunk his drugged coffee she'd given him that morning? She giggled to herself because she finally had access to his office. Now she could really get down to work. She was alone at last.

Twenty minutes later, Jake's mother Debra looked out the living room window and watched her son sluggishly tread the sidewalk towards her front door. He looked very cold and weary. She'd been praying he would come and see her. Debra hurried out the door and met him halfway. She gave him a big hug and brought him into the house.

"Jake, I'm so glad to see you," she said as she took his coat and hung it in the front closet. "Please come into the living room. I've been terribly worried about you. The family has missed you. Why haven't you returned any of my phone calls? Even your secretary hasn't been able to reach you. She said you were out visiting your clients whenever I phoned for you. You must be freezing. Come in. I've got coffee."

Jake sat down on the couch. He rubbed his cold hands saying, "Yes, please give me some coffee. It's freezing out there."

"Dear, maybe you should buy one of those car phones, so we can reach you."

"Mom, car phones are very expensive and I don't have that kind of money. I've been a fool. It's like I've been underwater for the last few weeks. I've had trouble rising back to the surface to get air."

His mother replied, "Hang on a moment. Let me get you some steaming hot coffee."

She went to the kitchen, and poured both of them a cup. He really did seem worn down and exhausted.

Lord, he really needs you. Give me the right words to say, she prayed silently.

Jake took a sip of coffee. Looking down at the carpet, he said, "I don't know how to tell you this, but I've been living with a young woman named Rue Smith. At first, I thought she was wonderful. But I've become exhausted, trying to keep pace with her schedule. Whenever I thought of phoning you, she was right there asking me something about work or taking me out to another bar. I'm beginning to wonder if she's been drugging me. I've had trouble remembering things. That first night at the hotel, I can't even remember how I happened to be in her room."

His mother continued to gaze at him. She took a sip of coffee and said quietly, "Jake, it's awful you've left your family for this woman. I'm very disappointed in you. Vicki phoned me a few days ago, so I already knew about this."

"I know, Mom, I can't believe she got me under her control like this."

"What if you're right, and this woman's been drugging you? Is this why you are so tired and confused? Is she doing something at your office with the files, or stealing info from your clients? You better get an auditor in there and make sure everything is fine at your office."

Looking very grave, Jake said, "I think you're right about work, Mom. Something seems off with Rue. She's always at the office till eight or nine every night working on the computer files. Only on weekends does she take a break. Jonathan Westly never stayed late except during tax season. I agree, I'd better get an auditor in there as soon as possible to make sure everything is correct in the business files."

"Good. Did you also know your wife has run out of money, and hasn't been able to buy any groceries? She finally told me this, so I lent her some money. The groceries cost $80. You haven't answered any of her phone calls. How could you be so cruel?"

Jake looked embarrassed. "Okay, I'll pay you back, and give you some money for Vicki. What could I possibly say to Vicki? Do you think she'd be willing to see me? I guess I could try phoning her."

His mother replied gently while she took his hand, "Jake, I will ask Vicki but I don't think she'll want to talk to you at this point. She is very angry at you. You've hurt her deeply and all of your family. Maybe later, she will let you see the children, if I'm there with you. But there are no guarantees. The first thing you need to do is get out of that woman's loft and stay here tonight."

Jake studied the carpet again. It was hard for him to believe he had been so thick-headed.

"I really miss the children. As I said, it seems like I've been in a fog for at least two weeks. I'm starting to think you could be right. Maybe Rue has drugged me with something. I'd better go to the doctor tomorrow and get checked out. You're right about not going back to Rue's place. Thanks for letting me sleep here tonight. She threatened to cut me off if I went to see my family. Rue already told me to not bother to come back tonight to her place, and swore at me."

With tears in her eyes, his mother said shakily, "Oh, Jake, I'm so glad you'll stay here tonight. I'll phone Sandy Brown, and see if she can get an appointment for you with Dr. Morgan tomorrow morning. We need to identify if you have any drugs in your system. You know, I think I have some of your dad's pajamas you can wear. I wish your dad was still alive so he could help us. He would know what to do."

Finishing her cup of coffee, she took the tray with the empty mugs and carried it back to the kitchen. His mother returned to the living room, after wiping her eyes with a tissue. She beckoned Jake to come upstairs with her to the bedrooms. Rummaging through her husband's chest of drawers in their bedroom, she was able to find an old pair of winter pajamas for him to wear.

Giving her a hug, he said, "Thanks so much, Mom. I really appreciate this and the clean pajamas. Good night."

"I'll phone Sandy Brown immediately and get you an appointment for tomorrow morning. It's ten which is a bit late but she knows I wouldn't phone unless it was an emergency. Good night, son."

He was glad to sleep in his old bedroom again. The single bed wasn't very comfortable, but at least he was alone in it. No one was there in the room to bother him, apart from his guilty conscience. It was relaxing to be back in his childhood home and remember the good times he had there. Jake felt safe. But he really missed his dad. If only his dad was still alive, he could tell him about the mess he had made of things. His dad would know what to do. When he finally fell asleep, he slept solidly for eight hours.

The next morning at nine, Jake phoned the medical clinic to confirm his appointment. Sandy had made it possible for Jake to get in for an appointment with Dr. Morgan at ten. At 9:30, Jake phoned his executive secretary Laura, saying he would be late arriving at work due to a doctor's appointment. Arriving on time at the medical clinic, he waited twenty minutes before he was ushered into the doctor's office.

Dr. Morgan smiled at him and said, "How can I help you, Jake? You look very tired. How's your work and your family?"

Sitting on the examining table attired in a green paper gown, Jake felt embarrassed. He looked down at his bare feet and wished he could stay silent. He mumbled, "Well, Doctor Morgan, I'm sad to say I don't know how my family is doing. I've not been back home for two weeks, ever since I went to a Seattle computer conference with my colleague from work, Rue Smith. She made me feel great, like I was a teenager again. I've been living with her. My boys haven't seen me since before this conference. But now I think this woman may have been drugging me, because my mind is always in a fog and I haven't been sleeping well. I hired her for my business when I needed a computer expert. With my former partner moving to Seattle, she was his replacement. Can you give me some blood tests to see if there are any drugs in my system? I haven't felt like myself for two weeks now."

Dr Morgan looked carefully at Jake and said, "Okay, Jake. This sounds bad. If she has drugged you, please stay away from this woman from now on. Here are the requisition forms for the blood work. Please go to the lab as soon as possible and get this done. I will let you know as soon as I can what they find out. We will phone you to come in once we have the results from the lab. I hope you're feeling better soon. Okay, let's take your blood pressure and other vitals. Can you stay at your mother's house again tonight? You do appear in a fog, but that could just be poor eating and sleeping for the last few weeks with all your changes. You have also lost weight, so start eating better, please. Make sure you get those blood tests done today."

Jake said in a hoarse voice, "Mom has agreed I can stay another night. I'll get the tests done today for sure, Dr. Morgan. Last night I talked things over with my mother. Now she is worried that perhaps, Rue might be stealing from my company."

Dr. Morgan gently touched Jake on the shoulder, "Well, get the blood work done and phone the police today if you think this woman is stealing information from your company."

Jake slowly got off the examining table. "Okay, I'll phone the police, once I get into work. Thanks for your advice. Bye, doctor."

Jake got dressed, waved goodbye to the medical team, and headed over to the lab. After they took blood from Jake, he drove as fast as possible over the icy roads to his workplace. When he got to the office, at 11:30, Laura, his secretary informed him that all the computers in the office were missing. She had phoned the police department at ten when she went into Jake's room and noticed his computers were also missing. Until she had checked Jake's room, she hadn't realized all them had disappeared. The police officers were on the way, and should be there any minute.

Jake looked at Laura and said, "Oh, no. How soon are the police going to be here? Where's Rue?" He rapidly sat down in the soft cloth chair in the reception area.

His secretary, looking confused, took a step back from Jake and sat in the other chair, "I thought you would know where Rue is. The police should be here any minute. Rue didn't phone in to say she would be late. It's so unusual because she is always here by eight. I hope she's okay."

He squirmed in the chair and replied, "No, Rue hasn't called me, but I wasn't home. I stayed at my mother's last night. Maybe she tried to reach me at my home number. I'll call there and see if she left a message."

After going into his personal office, Jake phoned Rue Smith at her loft. Because there was no answer, he left a message for her to call the office immediately. As he walked through all the rooms, he noticed the workplace was looking very stark; there were no computers anywhere. Jake instructed Laura to send all the other staff home early. He didn't bother to phone his own home; he knew Rue would not leave a message for Vicki to listen to on the home phone. He felt a little bad misleading Laura about Rue Smith, but he didn't want anyone to know he had been living with her, especially if she had stolen information from the firm. How embarrassing!

Just then, the police arrived. The stooped, grey-haired police detective said, "Don't touch anything. We haven't secured the scene yet."

He signaled to the other officers to come into Broadmoor Financial Services Inc.

"Mr. Broadmoor, will you please look through your office and see what's missing. Remember, don't put your hands on anything. Have all the computers gone missing at Broadmoor Financial Services Inc.?"

Jake walked over to the detective, shook his hand and said, "Hello, I'm Jake Broadmoor, but I didn't get your name?"

"Hello, Mr. Broadmoor, I'm Detective Cassidy."

Jake nodded at him. "I've gone through all the rooms and can't find any of the computers. I didn't touch a thing in any room. Laura, did you touch anything?"

Laura looked at her boss and shook her head, "I haven't touched anything in the office. Except, I did phone you on the reception line. So, I guess my finger prints are on that phone."

The detective looked at Jake and Laura and replied, "After we fingerprint everyone, we'll know who we can eliminate. We'll need to have all your employees go down to the police station and get fingerprinted. I understand from your secretary that you sent them home. She'll need to phone all of them and have them drive downtown to the station. Jake, we need you to check all your files and see if anything else is missing. We'll look for a match for any suspicious fingerprints in our national database. Do you have any idea who might be behind this computer theft? Where were you at eight this morning?"

Jake replied quietly, "No, I was eating breakfast with my mother at her house. I had a doctor's appointment this morning, as I've not been feeling well for about two weeks. Laura, my executive secretary has been here since eight. According to Laura, only Rue Smith didn't turn up at the office today. But Rue was looking at the confidential Creston financial statements at the end of work yesterday. She was the last one here last night and she was acting strangely. Laura told me that when she came in this morning, the alarm was not set. If Miss Smith was the last one to leave our office, she wouldn't be able to reset the alarm since she doesn't have access to the code."

"Did anyone try to phone her? What's the address for Miss Smith, please? Sir, why would you leave her in the office by herself if you thought there was something strange going on?"

Jake's executive secretary walked towards the detective and said, "Yes, I've phoned Rue Smith several times today, but she's not answering. She's the new computer expert at our office. Normally she's here by eight. I'll check out her address for you, detective."

Urging the detective with his hand to come into his office, Jake closed his door.

"Detective, I ran out of the office last night because I realized I've made a huge mistake. I've been living with Rue Smith for the past two weeks and she's started to get on my nerves. It was my mistake to leave her here in the office. I'm now afraid she's been stealing confidential information from our computer files. I think you should check her apartment right away; I'm beginning to think she has conned me. I went and got lab work done today to find out if she's drugged me."

"Well, this is bad news. But if you suspect her, we better find her, as soon as possible."

After being fingerprinted, Detective Cassidy gave Jake the okay to look through his files. As he went through all his paper files, he noticed the Creston Mining and West Realty, Inc. files were missing. He would need to go home, look at his home computer there and get his backup list of all the files of his company. The rest of the paper files appeared to be fine, but with all the computer information missing, it was hard to know for certain.

The police went over to Rue Smith's loft and rang the doorbell. No one answered the door or the phone. Detective Cassidy went to a judge and was given a warrant to break into the apartment. When they came back to her place that afternoon, there was still no one there. A neighbor let them into the reception area and the elevator to the fourth floor. They knocked on the door again, but there was still no answer. One of the police officers broke down the door with his foot. Two officers with their guns out yelled, "Police," but no one responded. As they cautiously stepped through the door, they could see there was no furniture or anything else left in her loft. Everything had been cleared out.

Some of the police officers took the elevator down to the ground floor and walked around to the back of the building. While searching the trash bin behind the building, they discovered ten computers. Some of them had the monitor glass broken, but others seemed to be okay. They phoned Jake Broadmoor to come to the apartment and confirm if those were his business computers. It seemed odd that Ms. Smith would leave evidence of the robbery right outside her loft.

When Jake got to the apartment building, he went to the loft and saw there was nothing inside. As he walked behind the apartment building, he saw the police at the trash bin pulling on gloves, and taking computers out of the dumpster. He looked in the trash container, and was delighted to see all the missing computers. Rue must be the one behind this. Some of them seemed to be salvageable. His personal one looked like it might still work, as long as the food particles were cleaned off. The police officers took all the computers back to their station to check them out. They said they'd dust all of them for fingerprints.

Detective Cassidy came around the building. He came towards Jake and said, "I've been told all the other employees were fingerprinted at the station. Hopefully soon we will be able to figure out whose fingerprints are on which computers. We will check them all out back at the police station. If it looks like the computers were compromised or that information has been deleted from them, we will have FBI computer experts audit them. We'll also see whether there are unauthorized prints on any of the computers."

Jake gave a small smile to Detective Cassidy. "Thanks so much, detective, for being on top of this right from the beginning. I'm impressed with your quick action and thoroughness on behalf of my business. Please thank the other police officers as well. Thanks again."

Detective Cassidy grinned. "Just doing my job, Mr. Broadmoor. I noticed there's nothing left in the apartment. Did you leave any clothes here? Looks like she took your clothes as well as her own. I've phoned the FBI local office just now and they've agreed to help us. They'll check all the computer records and files, they're the experts. They've told me all the data, even if it's been wiped clean, should still be there, since computer hard drives always save deleted files in a separate area of the computer. As well, the FBI will get a financial auditor who is a computer programming expert to check out the computers to see what has been stolen. In a few weeks, we should know what confidential files have been stolen from your clients and from your company. Hopefully, we can find any money that was transferred if Rue Smith managed to send any to her bank accounts and give it back to you. But there are no guarantees."

Jake looked down at the ground and tried to feel confident. He needed to reach his mother. Now he wished he had a cell phone so he could easily talk to his mother. Driving all the way back to his office, he was able to reach her.

Debra picked up the kitchen wireless on the fourth ring. "How're you, Jake? Did you find out anything?"

"It looks like Rue Smith stole every valuable business file in the office. The computers were all behind her apartment in the dumpster. Because I was so distraught, I didn't lock the office after her last night. I didn't make sure she left the premises before I left. How could I be so stupid? Truthfully, I was feeling frightened by her and just needed to get away. Do you think she had an accomplice? How else could she have taken all those heavy computers back to her place? But it was funny she would leave them there just covered in food right outside her loft."

"Jake, I'm shocked. How terrible. Were you able to get the clothes back you'd kept at Rue's place? You can stay with me until things are cleared up for you at work."

Jake looked down at his blue shirt and whispered, "There's nothing left at Rue's place except the broken computers in the trash. I guess she got rid of my clothes and toiletries, too. I'll need to buy a few new clothes. Hopefully, Vicki will let me come home today and get some of my old clothes to wear. What an idiot I've been."

"Oh Jake, what a mess. I'll phone Vicki, and see if I can go and find some of your clothes from your house. I know Vicki doesn't want to see you right now. Come over after 5 p.m. and I'll be home."

"But, Mom, I also need to get my home computer. Can you let Vicki know I need to get it today and check my work files in my home office? I also have some backup business hard copies there. Will you phone her and arrange a time for me to pick up everything, please? Tomorrow morning, I need to go to the bank first thing and check to see if there are any funds left in my accounts there. Thanks for being so kind to me, Mom. I don't deserve it."

"You're still my son. I'll always love you. I'll phone Vicki for you. She told me today she doesn't want to see you. I'll find out when it is convenient for her to have you come by your house. This way, I won't need to go over. You can go and get your clothes yourself. I believe you still have a key?"

"As long as Vicki hasn't changed the locks, I still have my own key."

Five minutes later, his mom called him back and said Vicki had agreed to let him come over at four. Vicki and the boys wouldn't be home, but Vicki confirmed his key still worked. It was so good to hear he could stay at his mom's. What a relief! Jake didn't know if he even had any money left in his bank accounts. His mom mentioned as long as he wasn't living with Rue any more, Vicki had agreed to let the boys come and see him on Saturday at his mother's place. But the most important thing was to get some money, and make sure Rue had not compromised his credit card. He would need to go to the bank, and make sure he still had money in there.

Chapter 6

Five days later, Vicki was amazed how things had changed. Rue Smith appeared to be on the run.

According to Debra Broadmoor, Jake had never heard back from Ms. Smith. Vicki was grateful for that. Rue had scammed Jake by portraying herself as a computer expert on her resume. Everything on her resume turned out to be false. The police said she had programmed phone numbers into her car phone. When Jake phoned for a reference, it would automatically go to her car phone. Rue herself would pretend to be the reference. Who knew you could do such a thing with car phones?

The police were convinced it was Rue Smith that had stolen all the confidential client information from all the computers in Jake's work place. Her fingerprints were on all the computers plus one other set of prints. She had also pilfered money by writing fraudulent checks from Creston Mining and a few other accounts. Jake was in a bad way financially. Rue had taken money from his personal bank account while he was sleeping at her place, by making a copy of his bank card. She had looked at his bank code in his wallet. Fortunately, she had not been able to get into Jake's personal savings account which contained $20,000, enabling Vicki and Jake to still pay their bills. They had wisely purchased their house with the money Vicki had inherited from her parents, so there was no mortgage to be concerned about.

If things didn't improve, Jake's company would soon be bankrupt; he couldn't work without the computers. And now, the business community didn't trust him either. At least the auditors had proven he had not stolen any money or confidential information from his clients. Who knew if his business would survive?

According to Debra, Dr. Morgan had also told Jake that Rue Smith had drugged him with scopolamine. That's why he had so much trouble waking in the morning in these last few weeks. The drugs left him in such a fog that he didn't notice when she was stealing information. He would sit and doze while he waited for her to finish work at night as she was stealing passwords from all the computers at the office. Now the Spokane police department had temporarily closed down his business. Jake had no computers left, and his clients had all gone to other financial companies. The police were building a case against Ms. Smith. They were hoping to catch her soon and bring her back to Spokane to face charges of grand larceny. Therefore, they wouldn't release the computers back to Jake.

Vicki was conflicted when Jake came over that day a week ago to collect his computer and work files and all his other clothes. She made sure that she was at Sandy Brown's place when he came over as she was still so upset with him. It was sad to go in their bedroom and notice that all his clothing and other personal items were gone.

Her mother-in-law phoned her to commiserate. "Jake really seemed to be under that woman's spell. He said the longer he was with Ms. Smith, the more miserable he became. The doctor told Jake he thinks she put scopolamine into his coffee every morning. The police have found evidence of a residue in a coffee cup like the ones she bought for him at Reem's every morning. It had been left in the trash can behind her apartment the night the computers were stolen. All her food trash from her loft had been in that dumpster, too. Jake identified for the police Rue's yogurt and berry containers. The kind of yogurt she had bought for Jake also had scopolamine residue in it."

"How could he fall for this woman? When I knew him, Jake didn't even like yogurt and he liked to eat at home, not at restaurants every night."

"Yes, he really changed. But, in the last week I have noticed a big improvement in Jake. His eyes are clear and he looks rested. The medical personnel say his blood work is clean now. He no longer has drugs flowing through his body. It has been two weeks since the robbery. He is hoping to get back with you, Vicki. He says he still loves you. Seeing Danny and Johnny again has been a great joy for him. He has agreed to let you have the car, and he'll take the bus. So you can easily drop the boys off for a two-hour visit on Saturdays at my house. I'll bring the car to you tomorrow."

"Thank you, Debra. I can't deal with Jake's problems right now. I'm just trying to survive. Any time tomorrow after eleven in the morning, I'll be here."

The next morning at nine, following a sleepless night, Vicki sat pondering at her kitchen table. She phoned her mother-in-law on the kitchen phone. "I'm going to speak to Pastor Scott and see if he'll talk with Jake. Perhaps he can try to arrange a meeting between the two of us. My husband was thoughtless and selfish, but no one deserves to be drugged and have his business stolen from him. I'm sad this has happened to him. If Pastor Scott thinks it's okay, I might agree to have a meeting with Jake."

"Oh, that's great. I hope it works out for you, Vicki. I'll see you later today."

Vicki phoned Pastor Scott at the church office. "Hello, Mrs. White. Can I please speak to Pastor Scott?

"Who is this, please?"

"This is Vicki Broadmoor. Is the pastor available?"

"Yes, he is, just a moment please." The secretary put her on hold, pressed the button on her phone and sent the call to Pastor Brown.

"Pastor Scott Brown speaking."

Vicki clung tightly to her handset, saying, "Hello, Pastor, this is Vicki Broadmoor. I wondered if you would phone my husband Jake for me? I can give you his phone number as he is staying with his mom. I think I might like to have a meeting with him. Maybe you could meet with him yourself, first, and see what he says. I don't want to talk to him if he doesn't speak to me with respect. I'm not sure if I'm ready yet, but if you could be there at the meeting, that would make me feel safe."

"Okay, Vicki, I'll phone him and try to set up a meeting. But I think I need to meet with him by myself and see if he is truly remorseful. His mother was telling me that Jake has had a rough time at his business. She also said the woman Rue Smith is wanted across Washington state for fraud. You have been through so much. I'll phone you once I meet with him. If I think you and he are ready to meet, I'll let you know. But it might be too soon."

"Thanks so much, Pastor Brown. This encourages me. I hope I can eventually learn to forgive Jake for what he did to me and the boys. It's been so hard. But I do miss him. Thankfully, my mother-in-law has been a big help with babysitting and buying food for me and the boys."

"I'll pray God's will be done in your family. I know God wants the best for you all. Perhaps Jake will see what a terrible husband he has been to you and will truly change. I'm praying he will turn to Jesus Christ and not rely on himself to handle things anymore. Even if he does change, you need to go slow before you let him back in your house. He needs to have a repentance plan in place and accept the consequences of his unfaithfulness. How could he get tricked so easily? Was he watching porn on his computer?"

Vicki sighed deeply. "I don't know what he watched on his home computer. Jake would go in his office and lock the door. He wouldn't allow me to use his personal computer. It was locked at all times. He said it was very expensive. Also, he said he didn't want me to delete his work files, if I mistakenly pressed the wrong button. He said he didn't trust me with it."

"I'll talk to Jake. God bless you, Vicki. I can see God is answering your prayers."

"Thank you, Pastor. I'm going to phone Sandy and ask her to keep praying. It's great Jake has been seeing the boys. It makes them happy to hang out with their dad."

Vicki sat down at the kitchen table. It was such a relief to see how everything was starting to work in her favor. It was hard to believe things were improving when she thought of what it was like a month ago. Imagine, that terrible woman was on the run. She hoped that woman would rot in a jail cell for the rest of her life.

Vicki took a deep breath, let it out and reached the kitchen wall phone, "Hello, Sandy. This is Vicki. I can barely believe the news. I'm so excited. It looks like my husband is starting to act like his old self again. I asked Pastor Scott to arrange a meeting for us. He's going to arrange to meet Jake and see how he's doing. Danny and Johnny are happy now that they have been seeing their daddy once a week at their grandma's place."

"Oh, Vicki, what wonderful news. I know Debra and I have been praying every week for you that God would restore your family. It's terrible what Jake did to you. He needs to learn to give over control to God. You know it would be good if he let you have access to the banking account, or at least give you money for a housing budget so you can buy groceries and gas."

"Thank you for all your prayers. Things are definitely going better since I told Debra what was going on. She's a wonderful mother-in-law and I thank God for her. She made sure Jake gave me some money. He stayed at his mother's place the first night after the robbery so that woman didn't have access to his wallet again. So, he was able to make sure I had some cash by the next day. We are doing okay financially as she didn't have access to his savings account."

"Wow, that woman is very tricky! You are fortunate she didn't get into your house."

"Yes, she's an evil woman. I'm so glad she's out of Jake's life. My new moms' group at the recreation center has been a lifeline too. I can talk about all my problems with them. So many of them have had horrible lives before they started coming to the group. I now appreciate how good my life has been until this point. Jake was such a good provider. We don't even have a mortgage on this house. Perhaps the church could help my brand-new friends from my new moms' group with some food vouchers? Many of them don't have jobs or husbands."

"Okay, Vicki. We do have meal vouchers. Cornerstone Church would be glad to do that for them. We also have counselors if any of them want to talk about their problems. We have women that volunteer to babysit if someone is being counseled. Let your friends know. We're happy to help them.

"Vicki, I was thinking that Pastor Scott and I could pray with you at Cornerstone Church. We have been trained by the late Rev. Dennis Bennett and his wife Rita to pray for painful memories and ask God to heal them. What do you think?"

"I'll think about it, Sandy. At the moment, I'm still trying to get my life back on track. Maybe in a few weeks, Debra could look after the boys. Then I might come in and see what you mean about praying for healing for me."

"Sure, Vicki," Sandy agreed. "We'll keep praying for you and the boys. I'm praying that Jake sees how hurtful he has been. God has certainly got his attention with all the disasters he has had lately. Being a workaholic didn't save him from making poor choices. I'll talk to you tomorrow. Bye."

Vicki sat back in the kitchen chair and thought about her family. She really missed her parents who had both died in a car crash on the Wenatchee pass in a terrible winter storm. It had been five years since the tragedy. Because her mom was not able to have any more children, Vicki didn't have other siblings. Both her mother and father's brothers and sisters lived on the East Coast, and she was not close to them. Sometimes she really wished she could talk to her own mother. But Debra really felt like a second mother to her. Vicki was so grateful she had Debra in her life. If only Jake was more like his mother.

Chapter 7

On Thursday morning, Jim, the drummer, saw Jerry at his school locker. Sauntering up beside him, he leaned on the locker next to his pal. He started tapping his fingers on the locker next to Jerry's locker. Finally, his friend looked towards him.

Jim asked, "What's up, dude? Is your song done? I dig the words and the chords too. That tune's awesome, dude. And you play great. That red Gibson guitar, it's amazing. You've got some cool moves."

Jerry opened his locker wider, searching for his school textbooks on the top shelf.

"Thanks, dude. We still have some work to do. The vocal and the percussion tracks need to be layered onto the music tape. Sammy and I hope to get it done today. But if we can't, we'll figure something out. Maybe next music class on Thursday we'll get it done. Or we'll try some time after school. We're planning to send it as a demo to the local radio station here in Spokane. I guess we'll use the drum sequencer machine on the recording, since you can't do it, right? I can't wait forever for you, Jim.

"Whatever...I have to get my own song done first. We'll see."

Jim looked around to make sure no one else was nearby, before whispering in Jerry's ear. "I saw Sammy flirting again with Rick in my chem class. He really likes her and she's always giggling at his jokes."

Jerry moved away from Jim, put his hand on Jim's arm, frowned at him and said with a growl, "Don't go there, Jim. Rick's her lab partner, nothing more."

Jim frowned right back at Jerry, whispering quickly. "But she doesn't have to sit right beside him, and lean on his arm every time, while they do the science experiments."

Jerry's face went red and he got right in Jim's face.

"Get a clue, Jim. Don't go there. Just shut up! She's my girl. End of story."

Jerry bumped into Jim's shoulder. So, Jim pushed Jerry with his hand, right back into Jerry's open locker door.

Jerry shouted, "Hey, watch it. Don't wreck my shoulder. I still need to be able to play my guitar."

"Okay, okay. You started it. Let's not get in trouble with the principal. Sorry." Jim lifted his hands in a gesture of peace. "I'm just trying to warn you, buddy. I have your back. Don't be surprised if she dumps you, too. She did that to lots of my friends in the music class last year. You weren't here, so you don't know."

"Okay, sorry I pushed you too. I still want to be friends. But don't get in my face about Samantha, dude."

Jerry looked down at his feet and said quietly, "Samantha told me she's my girl, so I believe her. Don't say anything more. I don't want to hear it. If you still want to be my friend, just zip it, buddy."

Jim waved his hand at Jerry. "Whatever."

Samantha came over to Jerry's locker from the other side. When Jim saw Samantha, he sighed, turned away and disappeared around the corner of the school hallway.

Sammy gave Jerry a warm hug before letting him go. She liked him because he was so good looking with his sparkling brown eyes, long dark hair, and slim physique. Jerry reminded her of one of the rock and roll stars from the sixties as he was so handsome. At six feet, he was one of the few guys in tenth grade who was taller than her. He was really cool, too. It was awesome when he played his red Gibson guitar. She could tell Jerry was troubled about something. She had seen Jim just go by.

"Was Jim trying to tell you lies again? You look stressed."

Samantha put her arm around his neck. Why was he so stiff? Jerry's face looked hard and stony.

"I don't want to talk about it. Don't go there. Let's go to music class and get that song finished."

He moved away from her and started walking toward the music room. She raced to him and walked right beside him, pulling on his right arm to make him stop.

"I'm coming, but I still want you to tell me what Jim said."

"Okay, I'll tell you. But you won't like it. Jim said you have a thing going with Rick, your lab partner in your science class. He also said you flirted with most of the guys in the music class last year, crushing them when you dropped them." Jerry looked straight ahead with his arms crossed, not looking at her.

Samantha stepped in front of him, putting her hand on his arm. She gazed at Jerry with admiration, and responded quietly so only he could hear her, "Jim is just jealous. He's not cool, like you. He's short, fat, and boring. His only good thing is his long, curly, black hair. Just ignore him. You're the only dude for me, Jer.

"Well, come on, Jerry."

Samantha looked at him and tossed her long black hair while Jerry gazed at her, admiring her beauty.

"Jim's my friend, so I don't want to trash him. He can be very funny. You should see how awesome he is on video games. He was the first one here to hang out with me. He's a great drummer. I don't know, I guess he just isn't comfortable with you but he's still my bud."

"Well, Jerry, he doesn't know me, and he's dead wrong. I don't want to talk about it anymore,"

She walked stiffly into the recording studio, while Jerry walked in quickly behind her.

Jerry really hoped they could get his song finished today. He needed Samantha's cooperation to get it done so he had to be extra nice to her. Samantha and Jerry worked in the music studio for the whole hour on the vocal tracks. While listening to the tape recording, they stood close together, smiling at each other. Over and over, they sang beautiful harmony into the mikes until they sang it perfectly. He sang high and she sang harmony below him. They ran out of time to get the percussion track done. The good news was they had completed the instrumental tracks the week before.

Jerry asked the music teacher if they could use the music room equipment the next day, in order to get his demo song finished. His music teacher agreed they could use the equipment for an hour at 7 p.m. the next day, which was the Friday. Mr. Rushton would be there as well, writing out a score for the band. They all were pleased to get it scheduled and were hoping the song would get finished Friday night. It was agreed the one hour on Friday night should do it.

"I will see you tomorrow at 7 p.m. Sammy, you're the best musician ever. I can hardly wait. It's a date."

Jerry gave her a wink and waved good bye. Samantha gave him a grin and wink back.

"I have to go to my dance class now. Did you know your big sister Allie is in my dance class, too? She's really good at jazz and every other type of dance."

"Cool, I didn't know you knew my sister. For just a girl, she's great. She always has my back. You know she even found me a math tutor so now I'm doing much better. I'm actually passing my math tests, woo hoo. I guess the teachers in my old school in Seattle didn't quite have it like the ones here in Spokane."

He smiled, saying, "Look forward to seeing you tomorrow. Bye."

Jerry walked home, whistling. Samantha stood still, glancing back at him fondly. Then she hurried into the Arts building. She didn't want to be late for her dance rehearsal.

When he got home, Jerry intended to tell his mother about his appointment tomorrow evening to finish his song at the school. But he found her all stressed out because she didn't know where Allie was and she was worried. It was already dark out there. Sandy had been stalked and harassed by a school teacher in Seattle. She didn't want that happening to Allie. Her husband had spent a few hours praying with her about that trauma but it still made her fearful. Jerry was able to let her know that Allie was at dance rehearsal at that moment. Sandy was relieved, but still concerned about Allie. She was in a hurry to go into her office at work at that moment to finish some financial billing. It had to be done before the next day. So, Jerry babysat Charity. In all the excitement, he forgot to tell his mother about his Friday night recording appointment.

When Sandy arrived home, she discovered Allie was not yet home. Sandy was not pleased. Allie finally rushed through the front door just before dinner.

"Where were you? I'm so glad to know you are okay. Did you forget I was having you babysit for me today?"

"What? You didn't tell me you expected me to babysit today."

Sandy continued, "I thought I did. If Jerry hadn't come in on time from school, I would have been really stuck. I really needed you to phone me about being late. Jerry had to tell me where you were. It's still dark at 5 p.m. in February. Thank God, Jerry was here to help look after his little sister as you never know who might be lurking out there in the dark."

Allie hesitated and said, "I didn't phone because I didn't know I needed to be home right after school. Besides, it's too expensive for me to have a cell phone and there's no phone in the dance recital hall."

Her mother replied, "Because you weren't there to help with dinner, we're just having hot dogs tonight. I was counting on you."

"I thought I did tell you I had an extra dance practice today. When did you tell me you needed me to babysit? I'd have said no, because I'd already promised to go to this dance practice. You always say we need to keep our promises, so people will trust us."

Allie beckoned to her mother, waving for her to come into the kitchen, so she could show her something.

"Look, Mom, I'd put the dance rehearsal on the kitchen calendar. Why didn't you just check the all-encompassing calendar, like you are always telling me to do? Sue from dance class walked home with me today from the rehearsal. She's a great friend. We're getting ready for the Spring Fling to make money for the grad events at the end of the school year. The grad dance committee always needs funds. I'm sorry I didn't remind you about the rehearsal. I thought I did tell you. Hot dogs are fine to eat for dinner for a change. Why are you so stressed?"

Her mother was standing behind Allie at the fridge, "Oops, Allie, you're right. I have a lot of things on my mind, so I didn't think to look on the calendar. I thought I told you, but maybe I didn't."

"Okay, I forgive you. I can babysit after school tomorrow if you want, till seven. Then I'm going out with Lewis to a movie."

"What? When have you started going out with him? I didn't give you permission to go out to a movie tomorrow." Sandy paused. "I guess you're a senior in high school now, so we need to give you some slack. I know, we did agree you can date, if we know the boy. Lewis is such a nice boy, but I didn't know you liked him that way." Her mother giggled.

"Oh, Mom. Don't be silly." Allie laughed, holding on to her mother's arm.

"What movie are you going to see? I hear *Apollo 13* is an excellent movie. But it would be wise for you to check with us first, before you make plans. Once again, I regret I didn't check the calendar. It's true I've been very stressed lately. You're right, dear. Would you please forgive me?"

After Allie got the hot dogs out of the fridge, she put them on to boil on the stove. Smiling, she said to her mom, "Well, you know Lewis is in my English class and my math class. He's a gentle giant at six foot five. Plus, he's so good looking with his red curly hair, freckles, and great smile. He is very intelligent too, and I admire him for that. When he asked me to a movie, I thought, why not?"

Allie then looked down at the floor. When she looked up, her mother saw Allie had tears in her eyes.

"He has also kept me safe from that creep Billy. He doesn't bother me between classes if Lewis is around. I really don't like that dude. He makes my skin crawl."

"Allie, what're you talking about? Tell me about him. If someone is harassing you, please tell the school administrators."

"It's not just me. Some of my other friends have been creeped out by him, too."

Her mother touched Allie on the arm saying, "Oh honey, this is terrible. Has he hurt you?

Allie hugged herself, looking out the window into the darkening sky. "Mom, no, he hasn't hurt me physically. He was kicked out two months ago, but he still hangs around the school. Lewis has always protected me from the creep when I'm trying to walk to the other side of the campus. As long as Lewis is by me, I'm safe."

Her mother looked shocked and exclaimed, "I'm phoning the school now to complain about this person, Billy. What's his last name?"

Allie looked down at the linoleum floor again and said hesitantly, "I don't know for sure, but I think it's Smith. No, Mom, don't phone the school. I don't think the school administrators can do anything about him."

She pulled at her mother's arm to try to stop her from using the kitchen phone.

"Stop that. I'm going to phone the school, Allie," and her mother pushed her hands away.

Allie wrung her hands together saying desperately, "But, Mom, the office closes at five. I'll just be more careful when I go outside the building. Okay? Don't embarrass me. Billy talks dirty to other girls, too, when they walk over to the other school building."

"Allie, that's why we need to phone. We must tell the school authorities about this harassment."

"Mom, Lewis is big and strong. He's good protection for me and my friends if Billy comes around. Also, my friend Sue from dance class is usually with me when I go from math class over to the English and history departments in the other building. When I'm with my other friends, Billy doesn't bother me."

"Allie, I'm still going to phone the school, even if you don't think it will help."

Her mother walked away from her into the hallway and over to her husband's home office.

Hurrying after her, Allie stopped and said with exasperation, "Okay, Mom, but I don't think it will work. I don't get why you are interfering. My new friends at this school don't want me acting like a child. Don't treat me like one. Dial down, Mom."

Going into her husband's home office, Sandy shut the door, and locked it behind her. She found the phone number for Whitmore High School in the phone book, and dialed the number. The answering machine said the school was closed for the night. She left a message anyway. Before she started work at ten the next day, Sandy planned to phone the vice principal to make sure he got her message. Sandy planned to talk to Scott that evening as well to let him know what was happening at the school.

"Allie, you were right, the school was closed. But I did leave a voice mail for Vice Principal Stone. I'll phone at nine tomorrow morning and try to speak to him. It's not safe for you or any other girls to have this person loitering around the school, hassling you."

When they sat down for dinner, Sandy mentioned to Scott that she needed to talk to him in his office after dinner. He was busy eating his hot dog. It didn't look like he had heard her. When he finished his last bite, he looked at Sandy, giving her a nod. "Okay, Sandy, but I do have my sermon to get ready for Sunday. I'm on a tight timeline here. So please, let's not talk too long about whatever it is."

Sandy scowled at him, saying, "Don't brush me off, Scott. This is important. You 'll think so, too, once I tell you about the problem."

"Okay, dear. I'll make the time."

She turned quickly and smiled at all her children.

"After having only hot dogs for dinner, I think we deserve a special treat, don't you? Who wants chocolate ice cream for dessert?"

Charity looked hopefully at her mother. "Chocolate ice cream, Mom? My favorite. Yummy. What about you, Josh? Is it your favorite, too?"

Josh smiled at his little sister. "No, Charity, my favorite is Rocky Road. But I'll eat chocolate ice cream too." He looked at his mom, grinning. "Mom, can I have three scoops, please?"

His mother smiled back at him. Glancing at Allie, she motioned for her to come and help put the ice cream out in the bowls. When everyone had finished eating their dessert, Sandy organized her boys to do clean up and put the dishes in the dishwasher. It was very important for Sandy that all of her children took part in cooking and cleaning. She asked Allie to get Charity ready for bed.

Taking Scott by the hand, she pulled him toward his office.

"What's so mysterious that we can't mention it at the dinner table, Sandy?"

"Come on, let's go to your study and I'll tell you all about it."

Standing close together in the hallway, Sandy gave him a big hug. After going into his study, she firmly closed the door.

Sandy said to her husband, "First the good news, Allie told me today, she's going to a movie with Lewis Lee tomorrow night. That's a surprise to me, but he's a nice young man. I hope they have fun. But here's the bad news, Allie just told me before dinner that she's being harassed by a young dropout called Billy. When I phoned the school about it, they were closed, so I thought I'd phone them back tomorrow morning. I guess Mr. Stone's the one whom we need to talk to."

"I'm glad she's going out with him, but it's sudden, isn't it? I guess we'll see what happens there. I hope it doesn't interfere with the tutoring. This is terrible news about that guy harassing our Allie. We need to get on this immediately."

Scott brought a chair over for Sandy. He moved his desk chair around so he could sit right beside her. He gently took her hand. Sandy started to weep quietly.

"This is very troubling. I don't want you to have to rehash those bad memories from when you were 17. Why don't you let me handle this, Sandy? I agree we need to talk to the school administrators. I can take Allie to school early tomorrow, and see if we're able to talk in person to Mr. Stone. I will go speak with Allie about this."

Sandy looked puzzled as she wiped her tears away, "But wait, I thought you have appointments at the church, first thing tomorrow? I want to be involved in this school meeting, too."

"Sandy, I don't actually have any appointments tomorrow. I just planned to spend the day finishing my sermon. I already know Mr. Stone, so he might be more willing to listen to our concerns if I go to speak to him. If I bring Allie with me, she can tell him what's been happening to her. If the police are called into the school, they need to know the information firsthand from her. I'll certainly make time to take Allie with me to the school."

"All right, but I want to know everything you find out. Of course, I do have work tomorrow morning at ten. Plus, I feel very distraught about this, so it's true maybe you would be better at speaking with the school vice principal. But I really need you to phone me afterwards and let me know what happened in the meeting. This is very important to me."

The tears continued to flow silently down Sandy's face. Scott leaned over and gave her a hug.

"I promise I'll phone you, Sandy, as soon as I know what they will do to restrain this guy. He shouldn't be allowed on the school campus, period, so I hope this gets sorted out tomorrow. I promise nothing else will happen to Allie. This will not be like what occurred to you. I pray you will give those bad memories back to the Lord Jesus Christ from when you were harassed at age 17. Let him carry your heavy yoke, for he knows about your trauma and wants to heal you."

Scott went up the stairs to talk to Allie in her room. She agreed to go with him to talk to the school officials. He was troubled himself by his discussion with his daughter. Immediately going to his bedroom, he found his wife Sandy sitting there in her red chair, still tearful. Going to her, he hugged her as they tried to comfort each other. As he thought about his day, he remembered how his Scottish father and grandfather would say when he was a young boy, "Just buck up. Everything will work out. Where's your stiff upper lip?" His grandfather Brown had emigrated from Glasgow, Scotland in the early 1920s. Thank God his father was more willing to accept his family and his emotions after spending time with Dennis and Rita Bennett at the Friday night meetings in Seattle.

Even though it was only nine in the evening, they just needed some down time. Everyone was home in bed. After he prayed for several moments, they both fell asleep with their arms around each other.

As Scott was drifting off to sleep, he heard the Lord Jesus say to him, "I will be with you always, Scott. Do not fear. All things will turn out for the good."

Chapter 8

The next morning, Allie and her father went to the school office and asked to speak to Mr. Stone. It was still early, before classes started. They were hoping Mr. Stone would be available to see them before his other appointments.

The school secretary said, "Just a minute. I'll see if he's in his office."

Knocking on his door, she heard the vice principal say, "Come in. How can I help you?"

The secretary explained Pastor Brown was there again urgently needing to speak to Vice Principal Stone. He looked surprised but agreed to see Pastor Brown at once. The secretary came back to the main reception area and told the Browns to please go right in. Allie whispered to her father that she was feeling afraid, but her father encouraged her to come with him into the school office. He took her gently by the arm, marching into the office.

Mr. Stone was startled to see Allie there but gave her a smile as he said, "How can I help you this time, Pastor Brown? Is this your daughter? She looks so much like you."

"Yes, she does, but Allie is much better looking than me. Did you receive my wife's voicemail this morning?" Mr. Stone shook his head. "My wife learned yesterday afternoon from Allie that she's being stalked at the school by someone called Billy. We think his last name is Smith. He waits for her between classes and if she's alone, he stands beside her, calling her a slut and other awful names. This needs to stop. Do we need to get the police involved to put an end to this bullying?"

Mr. Stone was amazed. He paused and looked out his window. Turning to look at the Browns, he said, "I'm disturbed to hear this. This is the first I have heard about it. If it's Billy Smith, that young man has been expelled. I've seen him hanging around a little bit, but he has always been off the school property when I observed him. We'll let the police department know about this immediately. They'll probably want to speak to Allie. We can have the police officers come here to the school office instead of having to go downtown to the police station. The police usually bring in a female District Reserve officer to speak to teenage girls. I'll let you know when they come here to speak to Allie. Will that work for you, Allie?"

Allie looked down at her feet. She felt frightened and unable to focus. She mumbled, "I don't want to speak to anyone about this. But if it'll make Billy go away and stop bothering me and the other girls, I want to speak to the police here, at the school."

"Can you describe to me what this person looks like, Allie?"

"Yes, he's about 5 feet 8 or 9 inches tall with dark brown eyes and long black hair past his shoulders. He has a scar on his right cheek and wears his hair in a pony tail. I'm not sure, but he might have a beard. He always wears a black hoodie, black jeans and red sneakers. He's very dirty and smelly." Allie looked down at her feet, again.

She mumbled, "Can I go now? My English class starts at 8:30."

"Okay, Allie. I'm sad this happened to you. Please make sure your friends are always with you when you switch buildings on the school campus. I'll alert the teachers and get them to look out for you, as well. We'll deal with this at once. It does sound like Billy Smith to me, too. I hope to have a restraining order against him later today."

Scott felt very angry about this happening to his daughter. He knew he shouldn't think this, but he felt tempted to punch this guy. Unlike many people, he didn't have a gun and didn't believe in shooting people. But at that moment, he had the urge to do it. Once he arrived at the church office, he planned to phone his wife, and tell her what happened at the school that morning. As well, he needed to phone Debra, the prayer group leader, to pray confidentially for the situation. But before that, he would go back to the school office and wait for the police to arrive to speak to Allie.

Sandy arrived at her medical office 30 minutes early. Scott said he would phone as soon as he finished his meeting at the school. She was so dismayed this Billy character would be threatening their innocent daughter. It was hard to concentrate. She spoke to Dr. Morgan privately, and he agreed she could take a break when her husband phoned her.

When Scott phoned Sandy later that morning she said, "Scott, what if that guy attacks our daughter physically? I'm afraid for Allie."

"Sandy, I know you're feeling scared. We're all feeling that way but we'll pray extra protection prayers over her and encourage her to be careful. Now that the school is aware of this situation, Allie should be safe. They have put a restraining order on Billy Smith."

At the end of the school day, Lewis was waiting for Allie at her locker.

"Lewis, hi. How's it going? It's so great there was no math class today. I wasn't in the mood to think about calculus. Did you know I won the role of lead dancer in the Spring Fling? Isn't that awesome?"

He looked down at Allie's lovely face. She was wonderful and very beautiful with her blonde hair and blue eyes. He gently took her hand. She made him feel so alive.

Laughing, he said, "Totally awesome. I'm so happy for you. But, Allie, what about the other thing? Did you talk to the police?"

Allie looked down at her pink runners, "Yeah, the police talked to me about that guy Billy. A really nice police woman took down my info. I never want to see that guy again. They said they'll be searching as quickly as possible for him. I hope he goes to jail immediately."

Lewis continued to tenderly look down at Allie. "That's why I'm here for you." He put his arm around her. "I thought I should walk you home to protect you and keep you safe from that jerk. I wouldn't want you to miss our date tonight."

"Okay, I'm so happy you said that. But just so you know, my friend Sue is also walking home with me. I'd already arranged it. But she doesn't live right on my block, so that's great you'll walk me the rest of the way home. I don't want to talk about that jerk anymore. Let's talk about something good." With a twinkle in her eye she said, "Like dancing. I'm so excited to get the lead dancer part. In my old high school in Seattle, I was Maria in West Side Story last year. I've missed getting a chance to be the star."

He responded, "Sweet, Allie. I think you're a star already. Congrats on getting the lead today." Turning to Sue, he said, "Hey, did you hear Allie gets to be the lead dancer in the Spring Fling?"

As she walked towards them, Sue flipped her blond ponytail, smiled and replied, "You go, girl," as she smiled at Allie and patted her on the back. "I always knew you could do it, Allie. I think it's amazing you can do all those jumps and flips. You're much better than Samantha and Ruby. Maybe it's because they are tall and you're so small. You jump, flip, and dance better than all of us."

"Thanks, Sue, but I've had lots of gymnastic training. Besides, Samantha and Ruby are only sophomores, so Miss Winter isn't allowed to have them be the lead dancers in this production. It has to be a senior. And I'm 5 feet 5, so not that short. But I did think you might get the part as the lead dancer, since you're 5 feet ten inches and taller than everyone."

Sue shook her head, looked down and kept walking. Allie was walking very closely to Lewis and Sue was walking on her other side. She seemed sad as she dragged her feet and didn't look at Allie.

"No, I don't want the part. I need to have time to study for midterms. You know, I need to keep my grades high in order to get into college and I'm just getting over bronchitis. I don't have time for extra rehearsals after school and on weekends. Remember, I work at the Gap on the weekends to pay for my clothes and I get 15 percent off my own purchases. Besides, the money helps with my college fund. Miss Winter did ask if I was interested in trying out for the part, but I said no. We don't need two blondes competing for the same spot when we want to stay friends."

Just then, the three friends reached Sue's house. They waved goodbye to Sue as she ran in her front door. Allie wondered when Sue's father would be home to help with homework and the yard work. Sue was the eldest of a big family of six children. Her mother worked part-time while the children were at school. Each day after work, she had to rush back home to be there for her youngest son, Cliff, who was hyperactive. At nine years old, he couldn't legally be left by himself. Mr. Montgomery, Sue's dad, was a fisherman in Alaska, and only made it home when the fish were not in season.

As they walked away from Sue's house, Lewis stopped, turned to look at Allie and grinned. He took her hand again and started sauntering along.

"I didn't know if I would get to see you twice in one day. How awesome, I get to walk you home. You make me so happy."

Allie looked at him, and giving him a nudge with her arm said, "I didn't think I would be able to smile at anything today. You're good for me, Lewis. I feel safe when you're around. This is so great. I actually won the dance part. I have a great boyfriend. It's hard for me to believe it. I have wanted this part so much. I didn't know I could feel so happy. See you at seven. Are we taking the bus, or is your dad letting you borrow his car?"

He continued to regard her with admiration. She was so beautiful with her long blonde hair waving in the wind. It was hard to believe she had agreed to go out with him. Her tiny hand felt great in his large one. It was good to be alive.

"My dad's car is in the shop, so we'll have to take the bus. There's a direct bus route right down Center Street, on down Division and across the bridge and downtown over to the fancy mall. The *Apollo 13* movie doesn't start till 8:30, so we should be there in good time. I look forward to seeing you later, Allie."

As she walked towards her front door, he couldn't take his eyes off her. Lewis was on cloud nine. He couldn't stop thinking of her. She turned in the open door, smiled and waved to him. As she went inside, he still had a big grin on his face.

Sandy was sitting in the living room of their house. Allie was humming a worship song when she came into the living room. "Mom, guess what? I got the lead in the dance extravaganza we are putting on for the Spring Fling. It will be on the last day of school before spring break. I'm so happy. The choreography is sweet. All the girls will have to follow me to get the dance moves right. It'll mean I'll have to do some extra rehearsals after school and two rehearsals on the weekend before the production. I'll let you know when the extra rehearsals are happening. But my midterms will be finished before the rehearsals happen. I hear the music department is also having the song writers perform their songs. So maybe, Jerry will get to participate in the Spring Fling, too."

Her mother stood up, patted her on the arm, and replied, "What great news. We'll have to ask Jerry what he's heard when he gets home. I know he's going to the mall to play video games at the arcade after school with Jim, but he should be home around seven. Do you want a hot apple juice? It's still cold out there, even though the snow is gone. How did it go, talking to the police today? Are they going to track down this Billy person and charge him with harassment?"

"Just wait a minute, Mom. Slow down," said Allie as she drank her hot juice. Then Allie went to look in the fridge for something to eat, coming back with a piece of cherry pie. Sitting down on the couch, she gestured to her mom to take a seat beside her.

Allie gazed out the window at the beautiful blue sky, "The police told me they'd look for Billy and they'd improve their car patrols around our school. Unfortunately, if they can't find him, they can't put him in jail. I had a very nice woman named Janette talk with me from the police department. There was also a detective named Cassidy who was covering for another detective on sick leave. They told me I needed to tell Janette exactly what Billy had said to me and whether he had made any threats. The school has a restraining order against him. The police are going to look out for him and arrest him when they see him. He's now 18, so if they find him, they can put him in the county jail at least for the night."

Her mother looked at Allie, exclaiming, "I pray they find him soon. Hopefully we can get some of the other girls to tell the school officials what interactions they had with this Billy person, too. I hoped the police would apprehend him right away. Oh dear, I'll have to let your father know. Be very careful tonight and watch out when you go to the movie. We don't want anything bad happening to you, like what happened to me. I think your father will need to pick you up. What time's the movie over?"

Allie groaned and covered her face with her hands.

"Oh, Mom. Come on. We can take the bus. We are almost out of high school. Please don't make Dad do that. You know Billy has never bothered me anywhere, except at the school."

Her mother said firmly, "You must let your father pick you up, or you're not going to the movie. Lewis knows this guy is dangerous to you. Tonight, I think it should be fine for you to take the bus there as it will be early in the evening. There will still be lots of people around.

But your dad has to give you a ride home, or I'll worry about you the whole time. You haven't told me what time the movie ends?"

Allie touched her mother on the arm. Sandy turned and looked at her.

"Mom, you don't have to shout. The movie should be over at 10:30. I feel silly having Dad give us a ride. Besides, what happened to you occurred in downtown Seattle. You were all alone, but I will have Lewis with me. It's safe here in this smaller city. He knows about the threat from this guy, and we will be careful. I guess until they find him, it'd be good to get the ride home."

Her mother replied, "Oh, I didn't know I was shouting. Thanks for being adaptable and agreeing. It took me a long time to get over the trauma of being stalked by my teacher. I will pray you stay safe, and try not to worry about you. Allie, you know how much I love you, right, dear?"

Allie went to the kitchen, and took the leftovers out of the fridge to warm for their dinner.

Chapter 9

Sandy was relieved to have her husband and Allie back home safely just before eleven that night. But she hadn't seen Jerry since four that afternoon when he went to the mall with his music pal, Jim. Now she was going to have to tell Scott everyone was home safe, except Jerry. She was just about to leave the kitchen to tell Scott she hadn't heard from Jerry, when suddenly Jerry pushed the back door open. He had bruises on his face, and his shirt was torn and bloody. She was so angry at Jerry for being late that initially she didn't notice how severely hurt he was.

Sandy exclaimed, "Jerry, where've you been? I've been worried sick about you. Your dad was out at a church meeting. He just arrived home from collecting your sister from the movie theater. Otherwise, I felt like I needed to have everyone out on the street looking for you. Where were you, Jerry?"

"Mom, I'm not feeling good. Let me sit down, please."

Sandy looked more closely at her son again. "Oh no, what happened to you? Jerry, why are you bleeding? Let me go and get some bandages. Allie, please get some paper towels to wipe up the blood."

Allie said, "Sure, mom."

Scott made Jerry sit down carefully and had him show him where he was bleeding. His mother gave him a soapy washcloth to help him clean up his hands and face. She then put some antibiotic ointment on the cut, and bandaged his hand. As Sandy had him take his shirt off, she was relieved to see he wasn't bleeding anywhere else; he only had bruises on his abdomen. They didn't wash the shirt because they wanted to show it to the police.

Jerry said, "Around ten minutes ago, about five blocks from here, this guy suddenly attacked me. He jumped on my back. I knocked him off before he started circling in front of me. He had a knife in his hand, and threatened to cut my face if I didn't give my wallet to him. But since I was at least three inches taller, I was able to knock the knife out of his hand with my foot. I punched him in the nose and he hit me back in the stomach. He kept trying to kick me but he missed. The guy ran off with blood running from his nose onto his clothes. The bad news was he got my wallet when it fell out of my pocket while I was struggling with him. I also got some of his blood on my shirt."

His father said, "But why were you so late coming home tonight? We thought you would be home at seven."

Jerry, grimacing in pain, sat down on the chair. "Didn't I tell you I had a music practice? I meant to tell you. We needed to put the percussion track down on my demo song 'Peace for You.' I thought I told you about it yesterday. Then we had to mix the whole song. Mr. Rushton, the music teacher, said it was okay for us to come in tonight to get my song done. So, after hanging out with Jim, I went back to the school at seven. It took longer than I thought to finish it. It sounds really great. We didn't get finished 'til 9:30. Mr. Rushton stayed and waited for us while we finished in the music studio. After I walked Samantha home, we talked for a while, as we were so excited about finishing the song."

His mother said, "Oh, Jerry. I'm so glad you're alive. Who was this guy who jumped you? Did you know him? What did this person look like? Did the guy cut your hand with his knife?"

"Yes, he nicked my finger with his knife, as I was turning around to put my foot up to knock it away from my face. That's another reason why my shirt is bloody, since I wrapped my hand in the shirt. I'd never seen the guy before."

His mother replied, "Oh, that's why your hand was bleeding. Did you have any money in your wallet? We need to call the police right away and let them know about this attack."

"No, I only had my bus pass and five dollars, since Miss Bloom hasn't paid me yet for shoveling her sidewalk. I don't have any other ID in the wallet because I can't drive yet, and I never keep my social security card in my wallet. But do we have to phone the police? It's late now; I don't want to talk to them."

Allie gasped. "I thank God you're fine, Jerry. We didn't even know you were out tonight, too. Wow, I'm so glad you're okay, bro. You need to talk to the police so they can apprehend this maniac. Can I give you a hug? Oh, I hope it wasn't that Billy guy that jumped you." Allie turned and looked nervously at her mother.

"Thanks, Allie, but be careful hugging me. I feel bruised all over my stomach," Jerry said as he stood up so she could hug him.

His father looked worried. He noticed Jerry looked very pale. "I've just phoned the police and they'll be sending Detective Cassidy over to talk to you. He's one of the detectives who talked to Allie this morning. He's a very kind man. Jerry, let me give you a drink of ginger ale. You look very green. Don't faint on me, now. Please sit down."

Twenty minutes later, Detective Cassidy drove up to the Brown family's two-story, white colonial house. He was pleased to see Allie again, but concerned her family seemed to be targeted. The detective was also glad to see Pastor Brown. But he was perturbed it was the second time in two days.

Pastor Brown brought Detective Cassidy into the kitchen, "Hello again, Allie. Is this your mom? Can you tell me what happened?"

"Yes, this is my mom, and this is my brother, Jerry, who got hurt in a fight."

Mrs. Brown was very pale with tears streaming down her face. She and Allie each had a hand on Jerry's shoulders.

"So, Jerry, can you tell me in your own words what happened?"

Pastor Brown walked over to the detective and whispered to him, "Jerry wants to speak to you privately. Can we please go into my office where we can be alone? Allie and her mom are very distraught, and don't need to hear the story again."

The detective responded, "Yes, I was just going to suggest going to another room."

Jerry's dad, the detective and Jerry went into his father's office. Jerry proceeded to let Detective Cassidy know what had happened.

"Jerry, can you tell me what the male suspect looked like?"

"The guy was wearing a black hoodie, black jeans and red sneakers. He had a small goatee, long black hair and dark brown eyes. I think he was about 5 feet, 8 inches tall. But he had a stocky build and was very muscular. He said he wouldn't forget me." Jerry put his head down, whispering, "The guy said he was coming after me again. I think I saw a scar on his face too, only it was dark so I'm not sure. Then that thief ran off with my wallet."

Pastor Brown nodded to Detective Cassidy, saying, "That sounds just like Billy Smith that Allie described this morning."

"Yes, it seems like it. Allie didn't mention a goatee but maybe he just hasn't shaved lately. We'll find out where he's hanging out and pick him up for assault. It's a good thing you don't have any ID in your wallet so he doesn't know where you live. We'll let you and Jerry know when we have him in custody. I'll put an APB out on him in the Spokane area. Bye now."

After the detective left, Jerry's father gave his son a big hug. Jerry was shaking and really needed the hug. It was like he was going through delayed shock. Tomorrow they would take him to a medical clinic to make sure he didn't need stitches. His father gave him the cup of peppermint tea his mother had made for him.

"Take a drink of this to warm up you. I'm so glad you're okay, son. By the way, why didn't you tell your mother you were at the school tonight working on your song? She was very worried when she didn't hear from you. Is there no phone at the school you can use to call and let us know when you'll be late?"

"There's no phone in that part of the school. I thought I'd told Mom about this recording gig."

"Who's this Samantha anyway, and why did you walk her home? Does she live near here? Remember, you're not allowed to date until you turn 16. That's in another four months."

Jerry pushed his father away, rolled his eyes, put down the cup of tea on the desk and looked at the wall. "Dad, give me a break. You know about Sammy. Slow down. Too many questions. Everyone else in the music class has a girlfriend. I can't talk about that at this time; I'm injured. Leave Sammy Jones out of this."

His father looked surprised. With an embarrassed grin on his face, he said, "You're right. We can talk about it later."

Jerry was relieved. "I don't think of her as my girlfriend but she's a really good friend. She considers me her boyfriend, even though you won't allow me to date yet. Remember, she's helping me produce my song so I need to keep her happy. Samantha's a wonderful piano player and has helped it be the best one, I think, in the entire music class. I'm thinking of giving her credit on my song, as she's done a great arrangement for it. You'll have to listen to the demo tape. Sorry, I didn't let you guys know. I meant to tell Mom yesterday. I guess I forgot because Mom was so stressed about Allie not turning up. Then she made me babysit Charity."

His father touched Jerry's arm and gazed kindly at him. Giving him another hug, his dad said, "I'm so glad the demo for your song is done. But there's a reason why we don't want you dating at 15. Are you allowed to be married at that age? Can you drive a car at 15?"

"Oh, Dad, lighten up. I know I can't do those things yet, but I haven't done anything wrong. You know I always try to do the right thing. I remember what you've taught me. I'm treating this girl with respect. Can't you leave it?"

"But, Jerry, why don't you let yourself grow a little older before you let your life be complicated by dating girls? Once again, I repeat we don't want you to date until you turn 16. But the most important thing is that you didn't get badly hurt tonight. I'm so relieved and thank God for that. I pray you have a good night's sleep with no nightmares."

His father hugged him again, and helped Jerry stumble up the stairs. At his bedroom door, he stared at his father and shook his head. "Dad, don't treat me like this. I'm not a little kid. Give me a break. I've just been in a fight. I know I'm only 15, but I'm trustworthy. This isn't fair; I'm hurt. I really don't want to deal with this. I'm going to bed." He staggered through his bedroom door and slammed it.

Scott was glad Charity and Josh both slept on the main floor, so hopefully Jerry slamming the door didn't wake them. He slowly walked towards his bedroom, opened the door, reached for his pajamas under his pillow, and got into bed. Sandy was fast asleep, thank God. He didn't think he would get to sleep for a long time. These last few days left him feeling depressed.

Scott prayed, "Thank you, God, for saving Jerry's life tonight. Thank you so much Allie stayed safe today. I pray the police quickly catch this person and he will soon be put in jail. It is great Jerry didn't have any information in his wallet. Thank you that this guy doesn't know where

Jerry and Allie live. Lord Jesus, I'm so angry at him that I don't want to absolve him for what he did to my children. But I know, Lord, you tell us we need to or we become bitter. Then we become chained to that person in our bitterness. Lord, it's not easy to forget the pain he caused my family. Help me to forgive him. May there be some way our church could help him. Please give us a miracle and get him off the streets so he doesn't create any more victims."

While his father was praying, Jerry slowly undressed himself in his room, trying to not use his bandaged hand. Letting his clothes fall to the floor, he reached for his pjs. As Jerry got under the covers, he tried to remember all the good things that had happened on this day. He had finished the recording of his song, walked Samantha home and kissed her. Oh wow, it was an amazing kiss! That was so exciting. But now his hand was throbbing in pain. His face hurt, too. He hoped the Tylenol his dad had given him would start working soon. It was hard to not remember seeing that guy coming out of nowhere and attacking him. Jerry had never done anything to the guy, so why was he going after him? He hoped sleep would come soon.

The next morning, Detective Cassidy phoned Pastor Brown at 9 a.m. Scott picked up the phone in the bedroom.

"Hello, Pastor Scott. We looked all night for the male suspect and found him just after eight this morning, sleeping behind a restaurant. It was in the skid row area of downtown. He looks just like Jerry described and still had Jerry's black wallet in his backpack. His nose was swollen. Your son thought the guy's nose was broken. He had some bruising on his chest from Jerry kicking the knife out of his hand. His shirt was covered in blood, as well. The perpetrator almost froze to death, as it was so cold last night. Now we have him in our jail cell."

"Detective Cassidy, it's amazing you found him already. God must've been with you."

"Well, Pastor Brown, I don't know about that, but we're happy to have him in jail. The guard just gave him breakfast. The suspect was very relieved to get a hot cup of coffee. Jerry 'll need to come down to the police station, and look at the police lineup of prisoners to let us know if we got the right guy. He fits the description of the man called Billy Smith."

Pastor Brown replied, "I think Jerry's still asleep. On Saturdays, he sleeps in. I don't know how much rest he actually got. Can I bring him down there at 11:30? That'll give him time to get up, take a shower, and have some breakfast."

"Okay, Pastor Brown, we'll see you both then. Just ask for Detective Cassidy. I'll come out and bring you through to the observation room."

Scott gently touched his wife on the arm as she lay on their bed trying to sleep. She murmured and moved away from him.

"Sandy, are you awake?"

"No, I'm not."

"Sandy, dear. I need to tell you something. They think they've found the assailant. He had Jerry's black wallet on him. Jerry and I have to go down to the police station."

"Oh, wow, that was fast. Just a moment. Let me wake up here." She paused. "I hope Jerry's okay. You better take him to that medical clinic downtown on the way back home to make sure his finger is healing properly. He may need stitches. Josh has an indoor track meet today, and has already left with his friend Stu. The girls and I are planning to go shopping at ten for some spring clothes. There are some great sales on today at the downtown mall. Later on, we're taking Charity to see the movie *Toy Story*. It's supposed to have amazing graphics and a cute story."

Sandy got up and dressed in jeans and a long red sweater. It looked great with her dark hair and eyes. It was amazing to her husband how much Jerry's face resembled his mother's.

She looked happy and relieved. "Scott, what a miracle that they've already caught this person. I hope it really is him. You know, there are lots of transient people downtown near the homeless shelter. You might want to wait till 10:30 to wake Jerry up. I heard moaning in the middle of the night and knocked on his door, but he didn't answer me, so I guess the moaning was a nightmare."

Scott went up the stairs to his son's room at 10:30 and knocked on the door. There was no answer, so he knocked again. Finally, he started pounding on the door.

"What do you want? Just go away. It's Saturday, and I'm sleeping in."
"I need to talk to you. It's important. Please unlock the door. You haven't done anything wrong, but I need you to get up now."

"Why? I want to sleep in. I need more rest," Jerry mumbled through the door.

"We need to go to the police station. Now open this door." Since there was still no response, Scott took a straight nail and maneuvered it through the key hole until the door unlocked. Going over to the bed he pulled the covers off Jerry.

Immediately Jerry pulled the covers back up and put the pillow over his face. He muttered again, "Leave me alone. I'm too tired," and he turned away from his father.

Standing by Jerry's bed, his father started talking to him. He explained the police thought they had found the young man that attacked him. Detective Cassidy had said he wanted Jerry to go down to look at a police lineup to determine if this was the thief.

Pulling the covers back over his head, Jerry shouted, "Dad, I had a nightmare last night about the fight. I don't want to go down to the police station. I'm exhausted. I said, leave me alone. No, don't make me do it. I'm afraid to see that guy again. It's like I'm frozen and I can't breathe."

"Son, you need to get up now. You can go back to bed when we come home and you can sleep in the car on the way down to the police station."

Pulling the covers off Jerry's head, his father said, "Son, you have to get down there, or else they won't be able to keep this male suspect in jail. The guy won't be able to see you, Jerry, because we look through a one-way mirror at the police lineup. If this is the person who's been bothering Allie, we all want to get him off the street. We must get him to stop hurting you and her. Please help us out this way, son. If you want, I can pray for you first, to help you get over your nightmare."

Jerry closed his eyes and put the covers back over his head. He turned his body away and didn't say anything more. His father Scott looked down at his watch and saw it was 10:35.

"Jerry, you really need to get a move on now. I know this is painful for you."

"Well, I don't feel like going anywhere. I can't go down there and see that guy again. I'm really scared of this guy. The nightmare was terrible.

In my dream, the guy kept coming at me and slashing me over and over again. Finally, I yelled 'Jesus, help me' and woke up. I don't want to go down to the police station. I feel paralyzed. I have a headache. I can't do it, Dad."

"Let me pray for you, Jerry. Dear Lord Jesus, I pray you would cover Jerry with your precious blood, that you would go into the bad memory and take it away. I pray you can help Jerry to have the courage to come to the police station with me and make the ID of this perpetrator. I know, Lord Jesus, that you say you will be with us always. I pray Jerry can sense you with him. Lord Jesus, please help him feel the peace that passes all understanding. Take away his fear. Help him to be able to get out of bed, have a shower, get dressed and go to the police station with me today. Lord Jesus, let him know I'll be right by his side." Jerry took the pillow off of his head and looked at his dad.

"Okay, I guess, that made me feel a little better. But first I need to have a shower, some scrambled eggs, toast, tea and cereal. Can you make me breakfast, Dad? Do you have a plastic bag I can put over my hand so it doesn't get the band aid wet, if I have a shower? And Dad, please keep praying for me. As long as you are there with me, I guess I can do it."

"Jerry, I'll always be there for you. I love you very much."

His dad gave him a gentle pat on his arm and walked to the door. Just before leaving, he turned around. "Thanks for doing this, Jerry. You're very brave. I know this is hard for you. I'll go and get you a plastic bag. I've got your back, so don't worry. I will go and make you breakfast. Scrambled eggs are the one thing I can cook." And his father laughed loudly.

"Thanks, Dad, for being here for me. I'll go and get ready now. Do you have more medication for the pain?"

"Yes, I'll give it to you in a minute. But you need to wait four hours to have some more. I'll take you to the clinic after the police station. The doctor can let us know whether you need stitches."

"Okay."

At 11:30, Jerry and Pastor Brown arrived at the police station in downtown Spokane. Since it was early in the day, there were actually still free

parking spots left. They went inside and made their way to the front desk. Pastor Brown asked for Detective Cassidy. He came out immediately, and took them back to his desk in the robbery section. He signaled for them to sit down in the chairs in front of his desk.

Detective Cassidy tried to smile at them but couldn't quite do it. He was so tired from being up all night. It was a good thing there was always a pot of black coffee ready to drink. Since he didn't have a wife, he could work whatever hours he needed to get the case finished.

"Thanks for coming, Jerry and Pastor Brown. It'll take 15 minutes to get all the prisoners up the elevator, and into the police lockup room. So, can I get you a cup of coffee, or would you prefer water?"

Pastor Brown replied, "Jerry and I just had breakfast. Neither of us drink coffee, but water would be great."

Five minutes later, the portly detective brought them each back a cup of water. After answering his phone, he stood and looked pleased.

"They've got the lineup ready. So, let's take the elevator to the third floor where we have the observation room."

As they entered the room the detective glanced at them. Both father and son seemed agitated and stressed out. He walked over and put his hand on Jerry's shoulder.

"Don't worry. No one in the other room can see or hear you. The mirror is only one way. They can't see you from their side of the glass. We won't leave this room until all the prisoners have been escorted back to their prison cells. Okay, here they come. Look carefully."

Jerry reluctantly looked through the glass and saw six men. They were all lined up against the wall of the other room, appearing to be around the same height. Four of them looked older, but the other two looked much younger. He noticed that number six was wearing a black hoodie, black jeans and red sneakers. That person also had a swollen nose, bruises, and a scar on his face with a scraggly brown goatee.

Jerry looked at his dad and the police detective, "Number six is for sure the one who attacked me last night. I don't know his name. Maybe he thought I had money since I walked Samantha to her home. She lives in the rich part of town. I'm glad he didn't attack us while I was walking with her. I wouldn't want her to get hurt as well. He must've been following me for some time, but I didn't notice."

Detective Cassidy smiled at Jerry and Pastor Brown. He escorted them back down the elevator to the front counter. "Well, thanks for coming in. You were probably too busy last night speaking to your girlfriend to notice him. He hasn't told us his name and he had no ID on him. One of the other prisoners in the lineup says he thinks his name is Billy Smith."

Detective Cassidy shook both of their hands.

He added, "This other prisoner also told us he thinks Billy's sister is a scam artist. He once saw Billy talking to this beautiful blonde down by the homeless shelter. When he asked him who the sweet babe was, Billy said she was family. The other prisoner offered to help him with any big score he was going to make. Initially, he asked this other person if he wanted to help rip off a business. But when Billy later checked with her, she said she didn't want anyone else involved."

Jerry grimaced in pain from his injuries. He motioned to his father with his good hand. Scott noticed he looked very stiff and sore.

"Dad, I need to go now. I don't want to waste my Saturday at the police station. Let's move. I need to get more sleep."

"Right. Thanks, Detective. Let's go, Jerry."

They walked out the door of the police station and went to the medical clinic. The doctor checked Jerry's injuries and put two stitches in his pinkie finger. Jerry was relieved to go back home and back to bed. The medication was making him sleepy.

Detective Cassidy was sitting at his desk with his head in his hands. His desk was littered with so many files that he didn't know how he would ever get through them all. Behind his desk, there were neatly filed binders on the filing cabinet. Those were the cases that had been solved. At three, detective Cassidy phoned Pastor Brown at home.

"Hello again, Pastor Brown. Once we submitted his fingerprints, we were able to find the male suspect in our data base. It's confirmed that it's Billy Smith. He has been in and out of foster homes for years, but now he's too old to be in the system. The Seattle police have an outstanding warrant on him for stealing electronic parts in Seattle. We'll let the Seattle police know we've found him. He has no confirmed address. Once we gave him something to eat and a drink of hot coffee, he agreed to talk to us."

The detective looked around and holding the phone close to his mouth said quietly, "Pastor Brown, Billy admitted his sister is Rue Smith, and he agreed to help her steal the computers from Jake Broadmoor's office. Billy was very angry she didn't give him any money except $60. Once she left, he was so disgusted with her that he threw all the computers into her dumpster. Anything to get her in trouble. His sister had told him she didn't care what he did, as she'd already stolen the data from the computers. What could he do with wrecked computers? He didn't have any wheels so he had no way to move the stolen goods. He's promised, if we let him out of jail now, to testify against his sister, if we ever catch her. Billy wants revenge against her."

The detective rechecked his notes. "He admitted to attacking Jerry because he was so hungry he needed money for a cheap hamburger. It looks like we'll be able to keep him in jail because of his involvement with the theft of the computers. Allie and Jerry should continue to be safe for now. I will let you know what his public defender finds out at his sentencing."

"I'm so relieved. Thanks so much for keeping me in the loop. It's great you quickly found this guy and got him off the street. What a miracle. Allie and Jerry will be very happy to hear he's in the county jail. I hope he doesn't get out for a long time. My family will pray he doesn't bother any more teens."

"Well, I can't guarantee he will never reoffend, Pastor Brown. But at least for now, he's still in jail, and will be there for the foreseeable future. Maybe your God did help us get him off the street."

"I certainly think God was there protecting us. I believe Jesus Christ sent his holy angels to protect my children and keep them safe. We'll be praying for you, Detective. Thanks for a job well done."

"You're welcome. As I was saying, I'll certainly phone you when we know we have a date for Billy Smith's sentencing. The undercover police on the street were the ones who found him, so I'll let them know how pleased you are with the arrest. We rarely hear when people are happy with our work."

"Thanks again."

Chapter 10

Vicki's children had been unwell all week. She was feeling exhausted and sleep deprived. Vicki had been waiting to find out whether her husband had agreed to see the pastor. Not hearing back from Pastor Scott, she phoned the church. The pastor apologized and replied that he'd had three sessions with her husband Jake in the last two weeks. He said he was just going to phone her back when she'd phoned. In the future, he said he would make sure Vicki would be in the loop. Jake had agreed during counseling that the pastor could tell Vicki what he had disclosed to him. It turned out he did have an addiction to pornography. Whatever Vicki wore to impress him, she could never compare to the enhanced pictures of the women on the porn sites.

Jake promised Pastor Brown he was going to get a filter on his computer so he could lock himself out of the porn sites. The computer was to be brought to the church office so the pastor could confirm this. Pastor Scott was planning to arrange for an accountability partner to coach Jake. He confirmed he had a person in mind. He was also going to encourage her husband to go to Twelve Step meetings.

Pastor Scott said, "Jake is even thinking of going to church with you and the family. He's close to giving his life over to Jesus Christ as Lord as he hasn't had success in making it on his own. In fact, he admitted he has made a mess of his life. More good news. The FBI have discovered some of the missing money in a bank account in Toronto, Canada. So, some of the clients in Jake's business will be paid back a percentage of the money they lost. Since Jake has had to apply for bankruptcy, all of his employees at his office have lost their jobs. He's now taking a computer course so when he starts a new business, he'll not be scammed by anyone else. Somehow, he will need to get the confidence of the Spokane business community back. The police have asked him to testify against Rue Smith. They are hoping to find her soon. Jake has been devastated by his work problems. He's still living at his mom's house and hoping to see you, Vicki."

Vicki shook her head, looked down at her feet and spoke firmly, "No, Pastor, I've decided I'm not ready to see him yet. I still love him, but Jake has hurt me so deeply that it's just unthinkable for me to see him. It makes me so angry that he would let that woman trick him like that."

"I regret that, Vicki, but I don't have time to talk any longer. I have a scheduled meeting now, so I could talk to you later, perhaps tomorrow if you want to arrange a phone call or meeting. I'll ask the secretary to phone you back and set that up. Talk to you soon. Goodbye."

Vicki slammed the phone down in frustration. Immediately, it rang again.

Sandy Brown said, "Hello, Vicki, do you want to go out for coffee this week? I'm off on Thursday morning, if you want to come over. Or perhaps instead we could meet at the local coffee place called the Meeting Place. It's run by Christians. On weekends, Christian bands come and play. I really like the atmosphere there. Or instead, we could go downtown to the River Park Square and look around. I know there're some coffee shops near the mall."

Vicki took a breath, let it out slowly to calm down and said, "Thanks, Sandy. I think I'd prefer to go to the Meeting Place. I'll see you there on Thursday at ten. Debra usually babysits for me, so it should work. Where's it again? I have so much to tell you when we meet."

"I have lots of news, as well. Allie is going to be the lead dancer for her dance troop at the high school for the special Spring Fling. Do you want to come to that? It sounds like it'll be great fun."

Looking out the window at the beautiful, blue sky, Vicki replied, "Oh, that sounds good. How much are the tickets? Sometimes I like to take a break, but I don't have anyone to babysit at night. I was hoping maybe Allie can babysit for me. If I go to this Spring Fling event, I'll need to ask my mother-in-law to babysit for me. I 'll check with her and let you know."

"Okay. The tickets will go quickly with all the parents wanting to see their teens perform at it."

"Yes, but my mother-in-law's not always available at nighttime. I'll let you know soon. I'm hoping in the future Allie can help out as well. So, what do you think? I hope to get a part-time job next fall, once the boys are both old enough to be in daycare. Hopefully, I'll not always be dependent on Jake for money."

Sandy replied, "Oh dear, Allie is really busy at the moment. But in the summer, she will be off school until she goes to the local college here in the fall. I think she'd be glad to help you then. But until she finishes her exams and her dance recitals, I don't think she has time to babysit. I will check with her and get her to phone you. If you get full-time work this summer, maybe she could babysit for you during the day."

"Sandy, I'll have to think about that. I don't think I'm comfortable with that idea. My boys are still too young for me to work full-time. The boys have gone through so much trauma in the last few months that I don't think I'm ready. I have to go now. It's such a beautiful sunny day that I'm going to take the boys to the park. I hear them waking up."

"Have fun at the park."

Vicky responded, "See you on Thursday, and we can discuss this again. Maybe I could get some part-time work in the summer. I'll have to consider it and get back to you."

It was 3:30 so all of Sandy's children, except Charity, who was already at home, came running in the back door of the manse. Sandy hoped Jerry's finger was okay because it was hard to play electric guitar with a cut finger. He seemed to be recovering from the trauma of the last few weeks.

Jerry walked up to his mother, and said, "Guess what, Mom? I'm getting to sing my song at the Spring Fling. I'm so happy! Jim has agreed to play percussion for me. Sammy will play her synthesizer while I play electric guitar. Isn't that great?"

His mom looked quizzically at him, "That's great. But who's Sammy, again?"

Jerry frowned. "Come on, Mom. She's Samantha, and she's my girl-friend. Didn't Dad tell you?"

"Jerry, you know you're not allowed to date until you're 16."

Grimacing, Jerry replied, "Yeah, I know. At school, Samantha tells other people she's my girlfriend. But I tell her she's just my best friend. I don't say anything about it at school. Nobody needs to know my business. As soon as I turn 16, I will officially tell everyone she's my girlfriend."

Allie looked Jerry in the eye, groaned, and turned to her mother.

"Mom, Samantha's way too worldly for Jerry. She wears really short skirts and plays tennis on the weekends instead of going to church. She's really smart but flirts with all the boys. Her dad's that famous lawyer, Randall Jones. They have piles of money."

Glaring at Allie, Jerry walked up to his mother and took her by the arm. He made sure his mother turned around to look at him.

"Mom, she's not like that to me. I never see her flirt with any other guys. So, don't say anything else, Allie. Do you want me to tell Mom about you spending all your time with Lewis now, instead of your girl-friends? Don't go there."

"Okay, dial down. Don't you each have math tutor tonight? Please stop arguing. Your tutor will be here soon. We will talk about this later, with your father, after your brother and sister are asleep. Go to your rooms, and get prepared for your math tutor, please. Thank you."

Sandy put her hands up and physically intervened between her chil-dren. While muttering at each other, they both plodded up the stairs and banged their doors shut.

Three hours later, the math tutor, Lewis, finally left the Brown manse. He had already finished his tutoring thirty minutes earlier, but stayed later talking and cuddling with Allie. When he left, Scott and Sandy called Allie and Jerry into his office.

"Okay, Allie. It seems you owe Jerry an apology for talking trashy about his friend."

"Well, Dad, I thought you said he couldn't date. I was just reminding him of your rules. This girl Samantha tells all his friends at school that she's his girlfriend. Jerry doesn't say anything to disagree with her."

"Allie, we have had this discussion with Jerry already. He knows what he's supposed to do."

Each of them stood there with arms crossed, glaring at each other.

Allie was just about to speak again when her father raised his hand and said, "Allie, just listen, please. Jerry, you know you're not allowed to date her, right?"

"Yes, Dad. I told her I couldn't officially go out with her until the summer. It's not my fault she's told everyone we're an item. But after July first, we will officially be together."

Frowning at his sister, he turned and smiled pleasantly at his father and mother.

His mother added earnestly, "We want you to pass tenth grade, so we don't want you getting involved with this girl until after that. But isn't there a girl at church that could catch your eye, instead? What about Teresa? She's cute and I know she likes you. I always see her staring at you and finding ways to talk to you."

Jerry rolled his eyes at his mother. "Oh Mom, leave it. Samantha's the only one I want to date. She sings like a dream. Maybe, I could get her to come to church sometime. She'd be a great singer for the youth choir."

His mother nodded at him and his father smiled, replying, "Well, that would be a good idea for her to know about God. Does she go to church, Jerry?"

Jerry squirmed, "I don't know. Maybe she does. I will ask her. We mostly talk about music and her dance group. She tells me about Allie, and how Allie's always hanging around Lewis now, rather than hanging with Sue Montgomery."

"Okay. Thanks Jerry, for talking to us. You can go back to your room now. Please apologize to your sister.

"Allie, I was wrong to squeal on you. I'm sorry."

"I am sorry as well for telling on you. I'll try not to do that again. Will you please forgive me?"

Jerry replied, "Yes, I will forgive you if you can forgive me."

"Sure, Jer."

Scott added, "Allie, we like your boyfriend, but we don't want you to ignore your girlfriends. Sue really needs your support with all the stress at her house. Please don't snub her; she's been a good friend to you."

"Samantha doesn't know what she's talking about. I still hang out with Sue and Roberta from dance class. Lewis is just walking me to dance practice and waiting for me after school when I stay late because of that guy who was stalking me. Will they tell us if Billy gets out of jail, Dad? What if they don't tell us?"

Allie looked at her dad with fear in her eyes and started shaking. Her father regarded her with concern on his face and touched her on the arm. Her mom came over, stood right beside her, and started patting her daughter's back. Then Sandy found the afghan throw, putting it around her daughter's shoulders.

Her father replied, "It's been two weeks now, Allie, and he's still sitting in jail. The detective promised me he'd let me know if they let him out. They're trying to keep Billy in jail because they know he helped steal those computers from Broadmoor Financial, Inc. But until they find his sister, Billy Smith can't be a witness against her. I hope they keep him in jail indefinitely. Would you like us to pray for you, to help you feel better about those awful memories of him?"

"Yes, Dad. I still have nightmares about it," Allie replied. "I'm afraid to fall asleep at night because I don't want to have another one."

Scott closed the door, and motioned for Allie and Sandy to come and stand by him.

As Scott placed his hand on Allie's back, he said, "Sandy, please put your hand on Allie's shoulder. Jesus Christ, once again we pray your blood protection over Allie. We pray you would pour your light into those scary memories she has. May she sense you with her, Lord Jesus. We ask she will feel the peace that passes understanding that you give us, Lord Jesus. I ask you to cleanse those memories and the nightmares she's been having. May she have a great sleep tonight. I believe and declare she will have peace for the rest of this week at school and at her dance rehearsals. We thank you that Lewis wants to protect her. Bless our family, Lord Jesus, and thank you for protecting our children. Amen."

Her mother said with tears in her eyes, "Allie, read Psalms 3 and 4 over yourself at night. Psalm 91 is also a great spiritual warfare passage to encourage you and keep you feeling safe. You can read it to yourself out loud before you go to sleep,"

"We love you very much and pray you stay safe," she added, touching Allie on the back and giving her hug.

"Good night, Allie." Scott gave her a hug too. "Let's go up to sleep, Sandy, I need a cuddle."

Sandy turned to Allie and walked out the door of the office with her arm around Allie's shoulder. Scott came out behind them. Allie stiffly walked up the stairs, trailing her hand on the handrail. Sandy and Scott held hands as they plodded up the stairs behind their troubled daughter. They both hoped she would be feeling better soon.

Chapter 11

Sandy had started praying for Rue Smith as soon as she had heard about her. In every prayer meeting at church, the whole group asked God to help the police find her so she could stand trial on robbery charges. Lately, every time she had prayed about Rue, she got the word "Boise." She had heard this in her head at least five times in the last two weeks. She decided she must tell her husband. It was hard for her to excuse Rue Smith for all the damage she had done to her friend Vicki Broadmoor's marriage. But Scott encouraged Sandy to forgive Rue. He reminded her Jesus Christ said in Matthew 17 that people need to forgive each other, so she was trying to do it. But it was so hard. It was not a quick fix. Some days she'd had to forgive Rue Smith three times. She had also had to forgive Jake and even Vicki for allowing their marriage to fall apart, since they initially refused to have any counseling.

What if Boise was where Ms. Smith was born? The Lord Jesus kept whispering in her mind, "Boise," when she prayed about her. Sandy thought it must be Boise, Idaho, but who knew? She didn't know if there was another Boise somewhere else in the United States. Sandy was planning to ask her husband what he thought it meant. She knew there was an APB out for this young woman. God had given her information about things in the past so Sandy hoped she was hearing correctly this time, too. It would be so easy if somehow Rue was there in Boise just waiting to be arrested.

Another time, about six years ago while they still lived in Seattle, God had told Sandy where a kidnap victim was being held. God said it was on a street called Ash, in a place called Mt. Vernon. When she told Scott what she had heard from the Lord Jesus, he said she needed to tell the police. Sandy felt embarrassed, so he had phoned the police instead. Because they were at their wit's end trying to find this girl, they were interested to check this tip out. It had been two weeks she had been gone. When the police talked to the neighbors on Ash Street in the town of Mt. Vernon, they mentioned they were suspicious of the man that owned the blue house. He never came out during the day, only at night. No one knew this man. He never returned their greetings and was always very quiet when he left his house.

When the police heard this from the neighbors, they did a stakeout of that house and saw the man bringing out large black trash bags at three in the morning. The next day the police got a search warrant and found lots of trash in his bins and some suspicious lengths of cloth with blood on them. They were able to break in and find the little girl chained in the basement of the house. She was still wearing the same clothes from two weeks before. She had lost weight and was very dehydrated. Sandy was so glad she had listened to the Lord Jesus that time. The man admitted he had killed other children. Two days later the police had found the graves of three other little children and now that man was in prison for the rest of his life. The sweet little five-year-old had survived and gone back to live with her parents. Yet Sandy believed there was always residual emotional turmoil and post-traumatic stress when you were a kidnap victim. She wondered how that child was doing. Every evening she still took time to pray for that little one.

Sandy was told by his mother it was very difficult for Jake as he was now only working part-time. It was a good thing he was still living at his mother's place as he couldn't afford to rent an apartment. But it did give him the time to take financial and Excel computer courses for two hours every weeknight. Sandy was glad Jake had learned his lesson and, according to Debra, was not going out to any bars now.

She hoped somehow Vicki and her husband could get back together. The boys were really missing having their father at home. But Vicki seemed to be getting stronger and was not leaning on Jake much anymore, except for financial help.

When Sandy had been devastated after losing her parents three years ago to a drunk driver, her husband had noticed how depressed and sad she was. A year ago, Scott had heard about the amazing happenings at the Toronto Airport Vineyard in Canada. He had persuaded Sandy to go with him. So, Sandy, Scott and their friend Brianna from Seattle had all gone there to get a touch from God. Scott's folks had agreed to stay home with the children. At the Airport Vineyard, the speaker had said if you were grieving for loved ones, "Just give it to God. Be brave and raise your hands in surrender, because Jesus Christ would like to comfort you."

Sandy had done this and had felt a great warmth come over her. She rested on the ground, lying there for a long time. Brianna and Scott came and put their hands on her head. One of the prayer warriors had come over and prayed over her, as well. This was what they called "carpet time." She laughed out loud for many minutes.

She heard Lord Jesus whispering to her. He had said her parents were fine in heaven and she could stop grieving for them. They were safe. He would care for her now and he would never leave her. It was important for her to keep praying for her own children so they could grow in the knowledge of Jesus' love for them. He also indicated he had important work for Allie and Jerry to do, so she should keep praying for them daily. Josh and Charity were going to be great worship leaders when they were older to show their generation how to connect with God. Lord Jesus said her children were going to help bring a revival to Spokane.

Jesus also gave her Isaiah 43: "Do not fear for I have redeemed you. I have summoned you by name. You are mine. When you pass through the waters, I will be with you. When you pass through the rivers, they will not sweep over you. When you walk through the fire, you will not be burned."

Jesus also healed her from the stalking memories and threats from when she was 17. Now when she thought of it there was no pain anymore. It made her want to help other women that had had that experience. Jesus had come into the memory and shone his white light on Sandy, making her feel clean inside. He said to her, "I am always with you. Call out my name and I will help you." She wished she had known this back when she was that teenager who was the victim. She had been too embarrassed to tell her parents and tried to deal with it herself. It made her sad that her parents did not know Jesus until she herself became a Christian at the age of 17. When she told her pastor, he was able to let the police know, and the teacher who was threatening her and other girls was fired. At that time, it was great to learn that with support, she could stand up for herself, and no longer be the victim. Until she met Scott, she never knew anyone who had proper boundaries, and still treated her with honour and compassion.

Her family name of Mueller was not always treated with respect. Sandy's grandfather had emigrated with his family to Pennsylvania after the first World War. He was five at the time. Even though he worked hard and was a good citizen in the Second World War, he and other German immigrants were suspect. Her father had been brought up only by his mother as his father was always away somewhere working. She was a very critical and bad-tempered woman. So even though he tried to be kind to his two daughters when they were children, the first comment out of his mouth would always be something critical or unkind whenever he would greet them.

Sandy's mother was kind to her and her sister, Hannah but trying to be perfect in all things was the most important thing to her mother. Her family had been in America since the 1800s but their family had also come over from Germany. Sandy now realized that her father had been unkind to their mother as well as his daughters. In the late 1980s, her parents went to hear Dennis and Rita Bennett and became kind and gentle, it seemed, overnight. This was what made it so sad that they were gone now just as she was beginning to really feel comfortable with them.

When Sandy got up off the carpet with the help of Scott and Brianna Jackson, she could feel a change. It was peaceful. Scott said her face was glowing. It was hard to stay on her feet. She was exhausted. It blew them away when she told them the word she had heard from the Lord Jesus. Scott said he was so glad she'd had that touch from the Lord.

She finally had admitted to them she had been depressed for the last two years because she was missing her parents so much. Her only sister, Hannah, lived in Chicago and she rarely saw or heard from her. Her sister had dealt with the childhood rejection from their parents by getting into drugs and living with several boyfriends. She thought Sandy, being a pastor's wife, would reject her, so instead Hannah rejected Sandy first. It made Sandy sad that her only sibling wouldn't speak with her. The sudden deaths of her parents in that car accident was such a tragic thing for the whole family. No one had been able to say goodbye to her parents and her children had had a surprisingly good relationship with Papa and Oma Mueller.

At the time of the Toronto conference, they were still living in Seattle and had never been to Spokane. Both were excited about the prophetic word that their children would be used to help bring revival to Spokane. Back home in Seattle, they went to the library and checked out the business, population and church statistics for Spokane. They decided the family would take a trip to Spokane that next week as it was summer holidays. Scott thought if he could find a church who needed a pastor, he would apply for the job. Sandy had never realized until now that she would miss her friends so much from Seattle. The good thing was that it was not so far away that they couldn't visit. Sometimes, before she had started working at the clinic, she would drive to Seattle during the weekdays and visit them. But now she had good friends here in Spokane so she didn't miss them like she used to.

Chapter 12

March 1, 1996

Things seemed to be improving. Charity's ankle was fine. At six years old, healing is often rapid from a sprain. She was all excited as she was going to be a strawberry in her dance number in the recital. This meant she only had a few dance moves before standing as still as a statue for five minutes. Because Charity was the tallest in the class, she was at center stage while the other girls danced around her. She was pleased she was going to have a painted red face and a stuffed, red body. Charity was sure she looked just like a strawberry in her costume.

In three weeks, Jerry and Allie would be performing in the Spring Fling show. They would be practicing Saturday and Sunday afternoon at two at the school. Jerry would wait for his sister until she finished all the dance routines and walk her safely home from Whitmore High School.

As part of his discipline for skipping school, Jerry was helping with the weekly free breakfasts on Saturday mornings for the homeless. His dad was coordinating this. He had finished two Saturdays of volunteering already. Josh wanted to help with the breakfasts, as well, because he loved being with his older brother. At only 5'7" tall, Josh looked like a miniature Jerry. Because he had track meets, he would not be available to help with the breakfasts.

During spring break, though, the two brothers were going to help clean things around the church. This was part of Jerry's discipline, but also counted towards volunteer hours for both the boys at their schools. They also were going to visit some of the seniors at their own homes who Scott thought needed extra help with their landscaping. He was trying to teach them to do good deeds for others. The Brown family were encouraged to serve Jesus Christ by helping other people as part of their Christian witness. The fruit of the Spirit was very important in their family, especially kindness, gentleness and self-control. But as Scott knew, it wasn't always easy to do.

Allie was all wound up about being the lead dancer. There were five routines she needed to know perfectly for the Spring Fling. They were doing different dance routines throughout the evening. She loved her role as the lead dancer. Sandy was busy sewing all Allie's costumes, as well as those for her friend Sue.

Sandy was glad Allie had finished her midterm exams. Allie planned to volunteer at the Seniors' Recreation Center for three hours per day, Monday to Friday, during the two-week break. She would get credit at school for volunteering. She really enjoyed working with the seniors, as it reminded her of her mother's parents who were eighty years old when they died. She really missed her Mueller grandparents.

Jerry had been passing all of his math tests. Even on the midterm, he managed to get a 70 percent score. With his other courses, he was averaging 80 percent. Of course, in music class, he made 93 percent. His family was happy for him. His parents had agreed Samantha was allowed to come over to their place right after school to practice the song, as long as Jerry's mother was home. They practiced in the living room so there wouldn't be anything inappropriate. Samantha seemed like a nice girl, so the family was hoping it would work out.

Josh was looking forward to the weather improving, so he could start running outside again. He loved to run the steeple chase in track or do the long distance ten km cross country race. For now, they were still practicing indoors. Josh's friend Stu ran all the races with him. They usually placed either first or second in all of the races in Spokane. In April, they were planning on going to Seattle for regional trials to see how they compared to other runners in the state of Washington. Stu's dad was very enthusiastic and was willing to drive them over to Seattle on the Friday night, returning on Sunday night, April 3rd.

The whole family was looking forward to Scott's parents coming to visit just before spring break. They were making a special trip east, to watch their grandchildren perform in their various activities. Charity was dancing on Wednesday evening before spring break. On Thursday afternoon, Josh was scheduled to run in the ten km cross country race. The older teenagers were performing on Thursday evening at 7:30. Scott had promised to cancel all his meetings so he would be there at his children's events.

Scott's father, Jacob, was also a pastor in the Methodist Church. Like his son, he had been impacted by the late Dennis and Rita Bennett. They had taught them to pray for the release of the Holy Spirit and how to minister to others for emotional healing. Jacob and Vera had gone to many conferences where the Bennett couple were speaking. They had even gone to the Friday night meetings with the Bennetts at St Luke's Church. Scott's mother, Vera, had especially enjoyed buying and reading every book Rita Bennett had written on how to help hurting people. Now Jacob and Vera Brown were nearing retirement, more and more people were coming to them for prayer ministry, with encouraging results.

Scott's parents, Jacob and Vera Brown, had a large following in Seattle and had written and sold many books across the US. Inspired by the example of Rev. Dennis and Rita Bennett, they wrote on forgiveness, repentance and ways to overcome traumatic events in people's lives. Both Scott and Sandy were hoping Vicki Broadmoor would allow Scott's parents to pray with her over the trauma with her husband. She had not been willing to meet with her husband, nor with Scott and Sandy for prayer, for that matter.

They also wondered about the possibility of Vickie seeing Kerry Andrews who was a gifted counselor and a Christian psychologist they had used themselves. There was a special fund at the church to help with counseling fees. Kerry had been having a good effect on both Jerry and Allie. They both said they were no longer having flashbacks of the incidents with Billy Smith. Now everyone in the family was getting along better.

It was now a happy time, like when they lived in Seattle where the children had had many good friends. The family was realizing it took time for the children and Sandy to adjust to moving to a place where they didn't know anyone. Thank God for the teenagers here in Spokane who were willing to welcome the Browns as their friends. Charity was at the age where everyone was her friend. She obviously took after Scott who now knew everyone in Spokane.

Chapter 13

I t was strange, thought Rue Smith, to be back in this little country house. The cold in February was mind-numbing, so it was great when March came in and warmed up Boise, Idaho. Rue had always liked the sunshine in this part of the world. The blue sky all day long was a bonus. She still missed her Grandmother Sheaves, but she would never miss her Grandfather Sheaves who had beaten them all and sexually abused Rue.

Her grandmother's maiden name was Smith and she liked using that as her last name, instead of Bittle. Her own father had never deserved even that strange name.

Daniel Bittle was a drunk who was always promising to change. But it never happened. After leaving them for two years her father had come home with a baby boy that he called Billy. Her father had insisted her mom look after his kid, since Billy's birth mom didn't want him. Daniel Bittle never treated his son well and only Rue seemed to care for her little brother. Rue's mom, complaining they didn't need another mouth to feed, ignored the little boy. Rue liked him but he was always getting into mischief, especially when Rue was at school. The little boy was unsupervised; Rue's mom was always high on drugs and their dad was always out at the beer parlor. When he came home, he would beat them, particularly, Joannie.

Her mom was so depressed and worn down from the physical abuse of her husband that Joannie's mother had said they must leave Rue's father and come live with Grandmother and Grandfather. Grandma Sheaves was a wonderful woman. But Grandfather Sheaves used Rue in a way no granddaughter should be used. They lived out in the country and the grandparents didn't encourage friends to visit. Grandfather didn't want the friends to figure out the bad things that were going on in that little house.

The teachers at school were impressed by how clever Rue was with numbers. Math was her favorite subject. When she was thirteen, she became pregnant by her grandfather. Her family made her quit school because they didn't want anyone to know she was pregnant. She and her grandfather were the only ones who knew the truth about the baby's parentage. The baby boy came early at seven months, and was stillborn. Rue was so young and small, she almost died from the hemorrhaging. Her worried mother paid for Rue's ambulance to the hospital. The doctors saved her life. But because of all the unusual sexual abuse, her insides were damaged. Despite her young age, they had to do a hysterectomy. She had felt sad and missed holding a baby in her arms, even though it was her grandfather's baby. But her mother told her not to cry, that it was good riddance the baby had not lived. Something in Rue's heart turned cold that day.

Rue went back to school when she was 14. Since she had missed so much, she had to repeat the eighth grade. But things started to go better for her. Rue was determined to do well in school so she "could make something of herself" as her grandmother kept telling her. In one of his rages at his wife, her grandfather fell down dead with a brain aneurism. Rue was 15 at that time. Her brother Billy, at age seven, was put into foster care since Rue's mom had ODed two months earlier. He wasn't related by blood to Grandmother Sheaves, so she didn't want to keep him. Rue tried to find out where they had placed Billy but it was difficult to keep track of him.

Rue did the only thing she knew would help her. She gained influence with boys through willingly jumping into bed but she wanted gifts or money in return. She turned out to be very good at sports and became a bona fide track star. This made the last few years of school very enjoyable as she was so popular, and only her gentle grandmother lived with her so she was safe.

Upon graduating from Redwood High School in Boise, Rue landed a job as a waitress at a fancy restaurant. At the age of twenty-one, she became a bartender which paid for her to go to college part-time. First, she got an accounting degree, before she went on to graduate with a computer science degree.

Due to her beauty and slinky style of clothing, Rue discovered that men seemed to naively trust her. CEOs of many financial companies couldn't imagine that someone so beautiful could be crooked. Five scams in five years was pretty impressive, she thought.

Her last scam was tough to leave. Jake was very sweet and she thought maybe she sincerely loved him. Why did he go back to his family? Jake could have run off with her to the Bahamas and lived happily ever after. When he left the office that night almost two months ago, she was so angry at him. Why couldn't he see what a good thing he had with her? She was very angry she had not made as much money as she deserved from this scam. The bank had stopped payments on the accounts, so she was not able to get all of the money out. Life wasn't fair.

The money she put in the TD Bank in Toronto, Ontario, Canada had suddenly gone missing. She didn't dare go to that bank, in case the FBI had figured things out and were looking for her. She didn't want to use her passport as they might catch her. Rue had used her real name Margaret Rue Bittle for that account. She hoped the police didn't figure that out.

While it had been fun escaping to the Bahamas, the police seemed to be closing in, so she had panicked and scurried back to the United States. As no one who knew her now had any idea about her childhood and the remote old cabin she inherited from her grandmother, she had decided to hide out there. She loved hiding in plain view. The police in Boise never suspected a thing. Cops were so stupid.

Chapter 14

Charity, dressed in her strawberry costume, twirled all around the living room dreaming of dancing like Allie. Charity's ankle was just fine. For five minutes right in the middle of the dance recital, she was the star of the show. Being the tallest in her age group, standing right in the middle of the stage, Charity didn't move, while the other strawberries danced around her. After the performance, the family went to the Dairy Queen, so everyone could choose their own favorite type of ice cream. Of course, Charity chose chocolate, and didn't understand why everyone else didn't want the same. Sandy was so glad her ankle was fine. She was such a sweet little girl.

After all the children were asleep, Scott and Sandy had a good talk with Scott's parents. They were pleased Allie and Jerry were going for counseling. They said a prayer together for the teen's events the next day and for healing for all the family members. The family was learning that it took time to get over trauma.

Scott was busy the next day running around visiting older members from Cornerstone Church. He didn't go into the church office at all. However, he did make sure to go to Josh's track meet to see him win before running to his next appointment. Sandy worked from ten a.m. to 2 p.m. Most of the nurses and doctors had tickets to see Allie and Jerry perform in the Spring Fling.

After work Sandy rushed over to pick up Charity and then Josh. "Look Charity, there's Josh," her mother said. They waved at him as he walked over to the car.

"How did you do in the race?" his mother asked.

Slowly climbing in the front passenger seat, Josh looked weary. Sweat dribbled down his forehead. Grinning, he said, "Mom, I won the race, and Stu came second. Dad was there and came to congratulate me. So, we are certain to have a placement in the big Seattle race as we placed first and second. My legs are really sore, but I'm so excited to have placed first. I broke the record for the ten km course."

His mother beamed at Josh. As rain was starting to fall, Sandy turned on the windshield wipers. She always worried the roads could be very slippery on a first rain from all the car oil when it had been dry outside for a while. She didn't want to have a car accident like her parents.

"Oh Josh, congratulations, I'm so happy for you. Your dad and your grandparents will be thrilled. I wish my parents were still alive, so they could see you race. It's great that your Dad's parents can attend your race in Seattle in April. They're going back to Seattle at the end of March."

"Mom, I wish you and Dad could be there as well," Josh replied and looked down at his feet. There was a silence in the car. Sandy didn't know what to say to her son, money was tight, but he'd worked so hard they should be there to celebrate with him. He was twiddling his fingers and looking out the window at the pouring rain. His mother felt embarrassed and surprised. Josh usually didn't tell her what he was thinking.

"Well, you know that Dad and I have to be here for church services. What would we do with Charity on the weekend? Maybe, we could find money for Dad to fly out early to Seattle on that Saturday. I'll discuss this with him, and we will try to figure out a way for your dad to be there for the race."

Suddenly the rain stopped, just as Sandy was helping Charity out of her booster seat. The yellow tulips on each side of the sidewalk were raising their heads to the sun. White apple blossoms were blooming on the tree in front of the living room window. The robins were chirping as they dug up worms in the wet grass. It was a great day to be alive.

Promptly at 7 p.m., the family were in the school auditorium eagerly awaiting the concert. The curtains opened. Allie was center stage in her beautiful red, white and blue spangled dress. The ten girls behind her all had glittering costumes like Allie's. At one point in the performance, she did a backflip, a teenage boy in in the dance troop caught her, and then he threw her over his head. All night long, her team came on to dance between the other performers.

After the poetry readings and band performances, it was Jerry's turn. All of the teenagers in his music class had performed their numbers. His song was the last one on the program. Jerry started the introduction to *"Peace for You"* on his guitar, Samantha accompanied him on keyboard, and Jim began to tap the beat on the drums. The song started quietly and slowly, but built in crescendo and tempo. Jerry sang the first verse solo. Samantha joined in with harmony on the second verse, as Jim began playing a louder and more complicated beat. On the last verse, everyone in the music class came out and sang with Jerry and Samantha. As the finale of the concert, Jerry's song made his mother cry and touched her heart. Scott was right. Jerry was very talented. She wished she had noticed this before.

After the concert, some family friends came over to the Brown house for soft drinks and dessert. Grandma Vera Brown had made two of her famous blueberry pies.

"Samantha, you played very well on Jerry's song. Your family must be pleased with you," Sandy said.

"Oh, thanks, Mrs. Brown. It's such a lovely song, and the chord progressions are so easy that I enjoyed playing it. Did you hear a radio station has agreed to play *'Peace for You'* next week, while we are on spring break? I'm hoping Jerry might get a recording contract from this opportunity."

Jerry came rushing over. He took Samantha's hand and held on to it.

"Yeah, Mom. I'm so excited. I just got the great news from our music teacher. Mr. Rushton said he'd phone me when he knows the time they will be playing my song. Things are looking better, right, Sammy?" She nodded her head in agreement.

Jerry gave Samantha a big hug. His mother was surprised Jerry would be so forward, but Samantha didn't seem to mind. She noticed they continued to hold hands. Just as she was going to complain to her husband about this, Allie's boyfriend came over to her.

"Thanks for inviting me for dessert, Mrs. Brown. Allie was awesome in her dance routines. I'm so glad Billy Smith is still in jail. We're both looking forward to having a real break on spring break."

Lewis and Sandy both laughed at this little joke. Looking earnestly at her, he said, "Mrs. Brown, I've agreed to work for a veterinarian over the break to see if I would like to do that as a profession."

"Oh, that sounds like a good idea. You need to be good in math and science in order to make it into a veterinarian college and you are! I hope you enjoy working there. Thanks so much for the good tutoring you've been doing with both Allie and Jerry. I think they might even be enjoying math now."

He turned red and looked uncomfortable. "If only the math teacher at school had more patience, all the kids would be able to do math if he would show each of them. Thanks again for inviting me for dessert tonight, Mrs. Brown."

Allie came up and stood beside Lewis. He smiled down at her and took her hand. She turned to her mother. "So, did you like the dance routines, Mom? My dance instructor let me do the choreography on that opening number. It was totally awesome to get to have that chance."

"Yes, Allie, that was amazing. I didn't know you knew how to jump and do flips like that. You know me, I was hoping you wouldn't trip and fall. I thought all the dance routines were wonderful. The dance team stayed together through all those difficult rhythms and time changes. Your dad was really impressed."

At that, her dad came and gave Allie a hug. He looked at her with admiration in his eyes. "I am so happy for you, Allie. I'm glad you have all these new friends who can support you in your dance dream. What a great job you did. I could see you've practiced for many hours. When I danced in college musicals, it was a lot of work but so fun and rewarding. Do you think you'll ever be able to do any singing at this school?"

Allie turned, looking up to Lewis, and smiled. She started swinging their hands together.

"Yes, Dad, right after spring break I plan to audition for the part of Belle in *Beauty and the Beast*. Lewis is also going to audition for the part of the Beast. I'm going to show him how to dance over spring break. I hope we're chosen."

"Oh, honey, that sounds just right for you. But can he sing? I think the Beast has to sing, too, right?"

Lewis looked embarrassed, replying, "Yes, I sang in my church choir. I sing baritone or at least that's what Allie thinks as I can sing high or low."

"Well, I'll pray you both get the parts God wants you to have."

Later, after everyone left, Scott's parents, Grandma Vera and Grandpa Jacob, said how much they enjoyed the evening. They were very impressed with the wonderful talents of all their grandchildren.

Chapter 15

Billy Smith was so happy. His lawyer had arranged for him to be released from jail when Billy agreed to testify against his sister, Rue Smith. Because the police had not yet found Rue, the judge had let him out on parole. Billy wasn't allowed to go near Whitmore High School, but that didn't matter to him. He'd walk wherever he wanted; the police couldn't control him. Nobody told him what to do. As long as Billy saw his probation officer every week, he was safe.

He also wanted to find that creep who broke his nose near Rosemary Heights. Billy picked up his check from welfare, and went to the bank to get it cashed. The social worker had given him some new ID, so now his last name was officially Smith rather than Bittle. He was glad he'd changed it from Bittle, as his father never did anything good for him, anyway. It was amazing. With new ID, he could actually receive his money right from the bank. Tonight, he'd try and get a place at the homeless shelter. But first he would go by the high school over near Center Street, and see if there were any hot babes he could talk with.

When Billy arrived at the school at 3:15 that afternoon, there was no one there. He guessed they had a day off as no one exited the doors, even though he waited there until four. When he came out of the forest by the school yard, the only dude he noticed looked awful. It was this slimy-looking guy with scruffy yellow hair hanging out from under a black cap. He had a dirty blond goatee. The dude dared to come near him and grab Billy by the arm. He knocked the guy's hand off.

"Hey you, loser, I've seen you hanging around here before. What're you doing here, today?" he said as he grabbed Billy again.

"Don't you want to make some dough? You look like you could use some new threads," said the long-haired guy with a smirk as he shook Billy's arm.

He angrily yelled at the dirty-looking guy, "Let go of me! What's it to you? Do you own the joint, or somethin'?"

The guy laughed and said, "Yeah, this is my turf. Don't you want the money? All you have to do is sell grass to the dudes and babes here at Whitmore High School. I'll give you $100 for every six ounces of grass you sell. You charge the buyers $10 per pinch of grass in 14 Ziplock bags."

"But I've waited here for an hour, and ain't seen nobody."

"Duh, don't you know? It's spring break. You'll have to go to the pool hall and the video game store to find the kids. So, do you wanna make the dough or not? When you sell all the dope, you give me $740, and you get $100. Good, huh? So, do we have a deal?"

"How come you get $740 and I only get $100? That's not fair," Billy whined.

"Lookit, I'm the one giving you the product and the money…but okay, here's a $70 advance to get you goin'. First, make sure you buy some new threads, because you seriously stink. What happened to your hair? Why's it so short? You look like you're in the army, 'cept your clothes are a mess. Make sure you buy somethin' that don't stink or the vice squad will smell you coming." The drug dealer pushed Billy in the back and said, "Get goin'." And he laughed at Billy.

He glared at the drug dealer but then he smiled. Buying some new threads was good. "Okay. I'll do it."

The yellow-haired guy smiled back. Billy shook the hand of the guy while in his other hand the drug dealer gave him $70. He gave him seven ounces of marijuana in another black backpack like the one he owned already. As he stared at Billy, he threatened him with his pointed index finger. He started to poke Billy in the shoulder as he said, "Remember, if you don't sell all the marijuana and give me my cut of $740 next week, I'll come looking for you. You wouldn't want to disappoint me, would you?" "

Billy scowled back at the guy, pushed his finger away and said sulkily, "No, I wouldn't."

The dealer grimaced again. "So, make sure you find me and give me my cut. That's the deal. You better not rip me off. I'll be here every

Thursday at 5 p.m." He pointed at the ground near the tree where they were standing. He started walking away, turned, stopped and yelled, "Call me Brutus, and I'll name you," he paused, "Yak."

Billy was pleased to get the $70 in cash. But he thought what a stupid name that drug dealer had, and he didn't like anyone calling him Yak. Billy shook his head as he waited for the bus. At K-Mart, he bought some black clothes and black sneakers. He looked in the mirror and thought he looked even better now that he had been forced to shave at the county jail. He was pleased his nose looked so good after being smashed. His broken nose and his scarred face made him look tough. The new clothes made him look really fine.

Tonight, he would stay downtown at the homeless shelter. But after that he could sleep outside again, as the weather had warmed up. He was hoping the police would soon tell him they had arrested his sister Rue. She had treated him unfairly, making him steal all those computers from Broadmoor Financial, but giving him only $60 for all his time and effort. She had stolen thousands of dollars, and didn't share any with him, her own brother. He would show her. She was going to be put in prison for stealing that money. He also needed to find the guy that broke his nose. Billy was going to get his revenge.

Tomorrow he would find customers for the pot. Making sure no one was around, he had buried the drugs near the school. Carefully covering the hole with dirt and tree branches, he was certain it was safely disguised. He would get up extra early tomorrow, take the bus back there, and get his stash.

The next morning the sun was shining by six, the sky was blue, and the temperature was mild. Billy was happy to find no one had stolen his drugs. He wouldn't take any of the drugs himself, as that was stupid. Plus, he wanted to make sure he paid back the $70 advance on time.

Billy wandered down the street until he found the pool hall but it didn't open till 2 p.m. He walked over to the video store and saw that store opened at 1 p.m. He still had five hours to wait before he could try selling the marijuana. Oh yeah, he could go looking for that guy with the long dark hair and brown eyes who broke his nose. He would walk the two miles over to the Rosemary Heights area and wait for him there. It was the last place he had seen that guy. The girl who had been with him was hot; maybe he could catch that girl and have a good time with her.

When Billy made it to Rosemary Heights, he hung out near the park behind the girl's house. He didn't see anyone in the area. Where was everyone? Did the whole neighborhood go away for spring break? The only people he saw were gardeners landscaping and putting bulbs in the flower beds.

Suddenly, Billy thought he saw that girl who had been with the tall guy who'd fought with him over the wallet. She was coming out of a house with an older, good-looking woman. The two of them drove away in a car. Now that he knew where she lived, he would check in on her later. He was looking forward to seeing her again. She was sweet.

Billy walked back the way he had come and saw some guys doing landscaping work on church property with a sign that said Cornerstone. As he walked by on the other side of the street, he realized, it's the guy who broke my nose, and maybe his little brother. If he didn't have that spade in his hand, Billy would beat him up. Too bad there was somebody else with him.

Chapter 16

On the first day of spring break, Scott received a phone message at his church office. Detective Cassidy left him the message, warning him Billy Smith had been let out of the county jail. Scott couldn't believe it.

Detective Cassidy had told Scott he had been disappointed by the bad news. Until late the night before he hadn't known they had allowed Billy Smith out on parole. For two days now, he had been out on the street. He warned Scott to keep his children close by and not let them outside on their own.

After he heard this message, he immediately phoned the detective back to complain of this lack of notice, telling the detective this was terrible news. That his family needed to be able to relax at spring break, and not worry about this criminal hounding them.

Detective Cassidy had also said they still hadn't found Rue Smith. The district attorney wanted Billy to be willing to testify against her. Therefore, to keep Billy happy, they had let him out on parole. He was supposed to check in with his parole officer every Thursday at 2 p.m.

As Pastor Scott got out of his chair, he realized he needed to phone the detective back again and tell him about his wife's word of knowledge regarding Boise.

"Detective, I might have some news about Rue Smith. This may sound odd, but my wife keeps hearing 'Boise' from Jesus when she is in prayer. I know it's weird, but have you asked the police to check if anyone in Boise might have seen Rue Smith? Maybe she went to school there when she was young? Perhaps she has friends whom she's staying with from her schooldays."

Detective Cassidy responded, "I agree it does sound weird, but it wouldn't hurt to check it out. Usually Rue Smith travels to the Caribbean or Los Angeles where she can blend in. It turns out she has scammed at least four other companies. When we put out a national APB on her, four different police forces mentioned they were looking for financial scammers who fit Rue's description: Eugene, Oregon; Bellingham, Washington; Redding, California; and Mt Vernon, Washington."

He then went on to describe how the female con artist sounded like Rue Smith, though in some of those cities her hair was red or brunette, rather than her natural blonde color. Each time though, she had used the same MO. He would let Pastor Brown know if they found her.

"I hope you find her in Boise," replied Pastor Brown.

He hung up the phone, ran outside the church, and over to his sons who were planting tulip bulbs in the flower beds.

"I have bad news. Billy Smith has been let out of jail, so be on your guard. Until the police can find a way to get him back in prison, Jerry, be extra careful. He may be walking the streets, trying to find you. Remember don't walk anywhere by yourself. If you need it, please ask us for a ride. We'll ask Allie to not be on her own either. The buddy system will be important for you to use now, right?"

Jerry and Josh both stood up with shocked looks on their faces. Wildly throwing his spade down on the ground, Jerry almost hit his brother with it. Yelling at his dad, Jerry said, "But Dad, why would they let him out of prison? He stole my wallet, physically assaulted me, and stole all of Mr. Broadmoor's computers. What are the police thinking? This is stupid."

Josh nodded his head in agreement. He put his hand on his brother's arm and cautioned, "Maybe we should go home now, Dad. Let's phone Mom at work. We need to let Allie know before she gets off her shift at noon, so we can make sure to pick her up."

"You're right, Josh. Good thinking. We'll drive over to the Oaks Senior Center immediately. After I explain what's happened, I think they'll let Allie leave early today. After all, she's not getting paid for it. It's only a volunteer position."

Scott Brown felt like he was a knight in the Middle Ages going to his castle and drawing up the draw-bridge. He had a strong desire to keep his family safe, by locking them in the house. Charity was with her grandparents at the zoo, while Sandy was still at work and would not be home till 4 p.m. She was working longer hours over spring break, while Scott's parents were there to help babysit Charity. After hearing the news, Sandy said she'd phone the prayer group from church and get them to pray extra protection over their family.

That afternoon Debra had a phone call from Sandy Brown. Immediately she asked Sandy if Pastor Scott had told the police detective yet about Sandy's word of knowledge about Boise. Sandy said yes, but also mentioned the prayer group should pray that they find Billy Smith soon, and put him back in county jail. She also suggested Debra could tell Jake and Vicki that Billy Smith was released from jail.

Pastor Scott phoned Vicki Broadmoor the same day. "Vicki, just a warning that Billy Smith is out on parole now and is considered dangerous. Don't go out at night by yourself, and always try to be with other people when you take the boys outside."

"Okay, Pastor Scott. Thanks for letting me know. I'll pray he won't harm anyone else and keeps away from your family."

"Thanks, Vicki. We're being careful. By the way, my parents are in town. Do you remember them? They are very experienced prayer counselors. I was wondering if perhaps my parents might pray with you, to help with the painful memories of these last few months?"

"No, thanks. I've decided I'm getting used to being on my own, so I don't need prayer. At least when I'm by myself, I don't need to worry Jake will cheat on me, again.

"Even my two sisters-in-law, Jane and Kim, have been shocked by Jake's behavior. They're on my side and refuse to see him. Though you tell me he's now actually sorry and accepted Jesus Christ as Lord and Savior, his own family still feel really hurt and ashamed by him. I don't trust Jake, and I'm not sure I ever will. How can he ever make it up to me? Talk to you sometime. Goodbye, Pastor Scott."

When Jake came in the door from his part-time job, he went looking for his mother.

"It's so discouraging that in less than three months, I've lost both my company and my family. It's so depressing. I couldn't imagine Rue, who I thought loved me, would treat me so poorly. How blind and wrong I was. Mom, I pray one day Vicki will forgive me, and let me make it up to her for all the pain I've caused her. Counseling with Pastor Scott has helped me to see how deeply I betrayed Vicki. Until she refused to see me, I didn't realize how greatly I would miss her."

He sat on the sofa with his mother and she gave him a big side hug.

"Life has become hard for you, Jake, even though we both know it's your own fault. It's so troubling for me to think about what happened to your business."

"Thanks for caring, Mom. You've been so great to me. I really do miss Vicki. What do you think? Will she talk to me on the phone? It's been a month now. Has she said anything about me to you?"

"I don't think she's ready to talk to you yet, Jake. She never mentions you at all and walks away if I mention your name. But I suppose you could try to phone her. If she hangs up on you, you will get your answer. Why don't you speak to Pastor Scott about it first and see what he says?"

Jake sat on the sofa, looking out the window. Tears were streaming down his cheeks so Debra got him some tissues and sat down beside him. "Okay, Mom, I'll ask the pastor. We need to pray they catch Rue Smith soon. I'm wondering if I will ever get my day in court to testify against her. It's bad enough everyone will know what she did to me. I feel ashamed and embarrassed about that, but I need justice. Even God talks about an eye for an eye and a tooth for a tooth. I need vindication."

Debra was sorry he had got himself in this mess. He had been so deceived! Only God could solve this. She would keep praying for a miracle.

"Well son, I've heard Pastor Scott told the detective about the word of knowledge Sandy received regarding Rue Smith. I'm hoping we'll soon have news that they've found her in Boise, Idaho. Why don't we pray? Lord Jesus, we pray the police will soon capture Rue Smith, and she can be brought back to Spokane to stand trial. Amen."

His mother turned, looked at Jake and noticed he had some light in his eyes. His face was shining and his body looked relaxed. Jake appeared to have a weight taken off his shoulders.

"Oh, Mom," Jake grumbled, "I so hope she gets caught this time and can't scam any more people. I was very wrong to hook up with her, and now I know I have no excuse. That felt good, praying with you.

Debra replied, "I'm glad dear." She stood up and gave him a hug.

Jake continued, "I wish I had been brought up to learn to pray. What do you think? Will they catch her soon? I find it hard to believe God would talk to Sandy Brown and tell her where Rue is living. How does she know it's God talking to her? Why would you believe Sandy?"

Debra said, "Well, Jake, Sandy has been given words of knowledge before. She even had a word of knowledge about how to find a kidnapped little girl, once. She had been missing for several days. The police saved her just hours before the man was going to kill her."

"Oh, wow, that's shocking. I'm glad they found the kidnapper before he hurt anyone else. It gives me hope for my situation."

"Honey, do you pray now? Things get better when we pray. I regret I didn't know the Lord Jesus when you were young and so didn't teach you how to pray.

"That's okay, Mom."

"We should let Detective Cassidy know how unhappy we are that they would let Billy Smith out on parole. It's unfortunate Sandy and Pastor Brown have to be vigilant now to keep that young hoodlum away from their children. How could they let him out after he stole all your computers, and assaulted and harassed the Brown children? It doesn't make sense to me."

"I find it disgusting they would let that brute out of jail. Mom, I wonder how any lawyer could get bail for a scum bag like Billy."

"God can still do miracles. You had a great childhood with a loving father, yet still you had a fall. I wish we'd taken you to church as a boy. Maybe you wouldn't have been trapped by that young woman. I hope they soon catch her brother, too. I bet Detective Cassidy isn't pleased they gave him parole."

Chapter 17

Detective Cassidy had decided to get up early the next morning and drive to Boise, Idaho. His associate in Boise had put Rue's picture up around the small city. Some people thought they had seen someone that looked like her but she had long black hair. When he got to Boise, he was hoping there might be a High School Yearbook, so he could trace Rue Smith. Was that even her real name?

The Spokane police chief had agreed to let him drive the seven hours down to Boise. However, he had not agreed to cover his motel expenses. Detective Cassidy was hoping to get what he needed, and come right back to Spokane without having to stay overnight.

At 3 in the afternoon he arrived at the Boise Police Station. Detective Robbins from robbery detail had explained that even though the school was closed for spring break, the high school principal was still in the city. He would meet them at the school in 30 minutes. Robbins also said they had looked up events from the time frame from ten years ago in the city newspaper. They had found a girl named Rue Bittle who was in a 1985 picture for winning the Idaho State High Jump competition. The picture looked amazingly like the mugshot that Detective Cassidy had sent them.

Detective Robbins said, "I'll drive you over to the school. It's only ten minutes from here. I hope we can track her down through those high school pictures."

When they arrived at the school, Principal Jennings was waiting to let them in the front door. He was surprised to hear about Rue Smith. He had been at the school for 15 years so he still remembered her.

"Rue Smith was called Rue Bittle back in high school. Something happened when she was 13. She missed almost a year of school in eighth grade. She came back the following year, and re-did eighth grade. Rue's family was very poor. Her father couldn't keep a job, so the family moved here to live with her grandparents and her father disappeared. Amazingly, she did very well in math even with all the problems at her home. I think that her grandmother encouraged her to keep up her school work."

Principal Jennings continued, "When she turned 15, her grandfather Bittle died. After that, she seemed to blossom. I think Cliff Wright would be willing to give you some idea what Rue was like as a teenager. I'll phone him. Here's the yearbook for the year she graduated. See, she was on every sports team and won the Homecoming Queen crown in her senior year. I'm not sure she had any girlfriends, but she was very popular with the boys."

The principal took the year book and showed the detectives what she wrote under her graduation picture.

Rue Bittle: *I'm going to leave Idaho and make my way in the financial world. I'm going to be very rich and happy.*

Detective Robbins spoke up. "Okay, Cliff Wright is a mechanic and has agreed we can go see him at his garage over on Pender Street. I'll take you there now, Detective Cassidy."

He shook the hand of Principal Jennings. They were careful driving, as the roads were still slippery and might have black ice on them. Cliff Wright was waiting for them. After looking at the picture he confirmed for them that Rue Smith looked exactly like Rue Bittle. He also revealed something amazing.

"I think I've seen Rue here in town in the last few weeks. It really looked like her, except her hair is black now. When she was in high school, she was a terrible flirt. But when her Grandfather Bittle died, she went wild. If any boy wanted to sleep with her, she let them. But they had to pay her in gifts or money."

"You know, she might be staying at the old cabin where her family lived ten years ago. Her grandmother may have given it to her as an inheritance. Perhaps the dilapidated old place is still standing."

"Can you tell us how to get to it, Cliff?" Detective Robbins said.

"No, it's very hard to describe. I could show you how to find it. What do you think she might do if you turn up? She was never violent when I knew her."

"We can't guarantee she will come quietly. Please, draw us a map. Perhaps you could lead in your car until the turnoff and we can take it from there. She has no history of violence. You need to head back home immediately, when you see us turn at the cut-off. Stay away, especially if you hear any gun shots."

"How exciting. Let's go. I'll let them know at the front desk I had to leave early today. I'm the boss so I can do that."

After driving for ten miles on a curvy, muddy road, Cliff pointed to a fork in the road and drove off.

"Now, see up ahead, Detective Cassidy, there's the next fork in the road. Turn to your right and then turn left about ten yards up that road. Through those spruce trees, you can just see the roof of the cabin."

When they got near it, they quietly got out of the car without closing the doors.

"You stay over there, Detective Cassidy. I'll take the right side of the house, and you take the left," whispered Detective Robbins.

Detective Cassidy snuck around the corner of the house, holding his gun in his two hands and looking to see if it was all clear. He heard, "Freeze, Rue Smith, this is the police. You are wanted on an APB warrant. I'm going to arrest you. Please come through the door slowly and quietly."

There was no answer. Detective Robbins gestured to Cassidy and pointed at the door. He counted with his fingers: one, two, three, and then he attempted to kick down the door. It was very thick and it was locked. Detective Cassidy thought he heard a window open. He ran around to the back of the small broken-down cabin. A hundred yards away there looked to be some kind of smaller building. He went back to the front door of the house and gestured to Robbins. Detective Cassidy whispered to him he thought Smith might have climbed out of a window. They went around back and found the bathroom window was open just a smidge.

Detective Cassidy said they needed to check out the other place nearby. So, with their guns held out in front of them they walked slowly and gingerly to the old, grey shed. They made sure to stay in the trees while they trudged up to the building which was in bad shape. They came up from behind it and rushed to the front and found there was no door. They looked on both sides of the shed and discovered a small opening near the floor. Both detectives yelled, "Police!" and knocked the hole larger with some wood lying beside the shed, hoping to get inside.

They heard a female voice say, "Don't shoot, I'll come out with my hands up. I don't have a gun. Don't shoot me."

Cassidy saw Detective Robbins cuff Rue Smith as she crawled out of the hole in the shed. Reading the charge against her, he reminded her she could get a lawyer or they would give her a public defender.

Rue Smith was dirty and musty smelling. With her black hair and awful looking clothes, it was a bit hard to remember the classy woman who had seduced Jake Broadmoor. She looked up and saw Detective Cassidy. She smiled smugly and said, "Oh, it was you, Detective Cassidy, who caught me. How's Jake doing? I really loved that guy, you know. He was so much fun. Why would he go back to his fat, boring wife?"

Detective Robbins locked her in the back of the police car and drove them all back to Boise. They locked Rue in a cell overnight. Detective Cassidy got permission to stay overnight, as well. Since he had caught his culprit, the Spokane Police Department would cover his motel costs. A deputy sheriff would come tomorrow to transport Rue Smith with Cassidy driving behind the prison truck. He wanted to make sure Rue Smith made it back to Spokane to stand trial.

Chapter 18

At four the next afternoon, Detective Cassidy phoned Pastor Brown's house.

"Wonderful news. We've found Rue Smith. Just like your wife said, she was in Boise, Idaho. She had lived there when she was a child. There was a cabin in the woods that she still owned. We now have her in the lock-up here in Spokane. So, we'll be out looking for her brother now."

"Well, Detective. I'm thrilled to hear this and my family will be overjoyed. We've been praying for her capture since the night she disappeared. I'll keep praying Billy Smith will soon be back in jail."

Billy had been shadowing Josh and Jerry for the last few days trying to find an opportunity to catch Jerry by himself. But Jerry was always with his brother or being driven around by that man. Finally, he was able to track them back to their house. It seemed to Billy the blond-haired man must be their father and worked at that church they were landscaping. After many hours of waiting, he saw their car pulling into the driveway of the two-story house. At last, Billy would be able to pay him back. He had found a bat in the driveway of the house directly across from their white house. It was a gift to him so he could get revenge. He was going to knock that guy's lights out, or die trying. Running across the street as fast as he could, just as a person was getting out of the driver's side, he walloped the person good. He was sure it must be that guy with that longish dark hair.

Scott was just going out the door eager to tell Sandy about Rue

Smith's capture. He saw her car arrive in the driveway. Just as he ran out the door, he saw this guy dashing across the street right at Sandy. As she opened the car door and started to get out, the guy accosted her with a baseball bat, taking a mighty swing and hitting her twice. She shrieked in terrible pain. Billy knocked her to the ground. Just as he was going to hit her again, she screamed "Jesus help me!" Running out the door past his father, Josh came to the rescue. Racing around the back of the car he started kicking at Billy's right arm. Jerry heard the earsplitting yelling, looked out the open front door, saw the problem, ran to the living room, picked up the fireplace poker and rushed out of the house.

Josh was still kicking Billy on his right arm, trying to get him to let go of the bat. Sandy was writhing in pain and sobbing hysterically. Billy turned around and tried to hit Josh with the bat, but Scott, after standing still in shock for two whole minutes, suddenly came to life. He grabbed the other end of the bat and started pulling it away from Billy. The neighbors, hearing the commotion, were all looking out their windows. Someone shouted they had called 911.

Scott tried to get Billy in a chokehold, hoping to stop him from hitting Sandy again. He was able to move him away from her as he was the taller of the two. But he couldn't get a good grip on Billy's neck, since he kept turning around in a circle. By constantly moving his head, the attacker was trying to stop Scott from getting a good grip on his neck. With his left hand, Billy was trying to hold Josh off him. Now Jerry came running full speed right around the car and straight ahead at Billy's back. He hit him on the right side of the head with the fireplace poker. Billy went down like a top-heavy stack of lumber. Boom.

Three police cars arrived with their police sirens blaring. The officers jumped out of their cars, their guns drawn, yelling, "Hands up, everyone."

Scott Brown and his two sons put their hands up. The police ordered Jerry to put the poker down which he did immediately. Billy was momentarily out cold, but started moaning as he lay on the ground, while Sandy was still writhing in pain. Two ambulances had just arrived. The paramedics buckled Sandy onto a stretcher, and immobilized her left hand and arm. They gave her something for the pain and she stopped screaming. Putting handcuffs on Billy, they placed him on a stretcher and took him away to the hospital. He had regained consciousness and was swearing at everyone, profusely. Detective Cassidy went in the ambulance with the assailant and told him to stay quiet. Billy ignored the detective and unexpectedly lost consciousness again.

The detective hoped Jerry wouldn't get in trouble for hitting Billy Smith with a deadly weapon. After all, Jerry was only protecting his mother. Billy seemed to be trying to kill her. While the mugger had still been lying on the ground, Jerry confirmed he was the same person who had attacked him earlier.

The patrol officers asked the neighbors if they had seen what had happened. Everyone agreed Billy Smith had started the fight and Jerry had been only trying to protect his mother from harm. Josh had merely been trying to get the bat away from Billy. Also, Pastor Brown was trying to protect his wife. When the police interviewed each of the Browns separately, they all gave the same account. The police told Pastor Brown that as soon as he had answered all their questions, he was permitted to go and be with his wife at the local hospital.

Since Jerry didn't hit Billy on the back of his head, the police didn't think he would die. Because the attacker was a very muscular and fit person, God gave them a miracle and saved his life. The paramedics were amazed that he was still alive. The Browns decided God's angels must have saved him, so he would be able to testify against his own sister.

Jerry and Josh were very traumatized, and scared of what might happen because of the fight. They had thought Billy was trying to kill their mother, so their adrenaline was really flowing. They were both crying and groaning. Allie stayed with her brothers inside the house, while the police checked out the crime scene. The good thing was they only had a few bruises on their arms from the bat being flung around wildly. Allie was praying that her family would feel God's peace. She was so glad she hadn't heard or seen the incident as she had been in the shower. This meant she wouldn't have to relive this scene over and over in her mind.

Allie had told her dad, "I'll let Grandma and Grandpa know what happened. I'll ask them to tell Charity an edited version. Also, I'll ask them to pray with Josh and Jerry over this trauma before they go to sleep tonight. Isn't it great our grandparents are here to be with our family? I think Chinese food would be a good thing to order for our dinner."

Scott replied, "Yes, order some food. That always makes the boys feel better. Don't let anyone other than my parents and Charity into the house. You can call your boyfriend, but only family's to be here tonight. I'll be staying at the hospital, until I know your mother is all right. Please call Debra Broadmoor, Allie, and have her alert the prayer group to pray for your mother and our family. Lock the doors. Your grandparents will be here soon. Thanks, honey, see you later."

Twenty minutes later, Pastor Brown arrived at the Trauma Center at the local hospital. The on-duty nurse said they had taken Sandy Brown into surgery. Her left arm and wrist were both broken. He wondered why Billy Smith would attack his wife; she had never done anything to him.

Four hours later, at 9 p.m., the surgeon came out of surgery and talked to Pastor Scott. While he was in the waiting room, Debra Broadmoor and his parents had come by and prayed with him.

His mother, Vera, stayed there with him until they heard the news about Sandy. Vera was very disturbed by this incident but she knew the most important thing to do was pray. She was busy praying under her breath. The surgeon came out to the waiting room. He looked relieved and smiled at them.

"Pastor Scott, it took some time to operate on your wife, as her arm was broken in two places. Unfortunately, her wrist was also broken. We put a splint on her wrist and a cast on her arm. She's awake now, so you can go see her. But she needs her rest, so only stay a few minutes. You can come see her again at ten tomorrow."

"Thank you, Doctor."

Sandy looked up when they came into the room, and murmured, "Oh, Scott, I'm so glad to see you. What happened to me? I thought I was going to die. Who was attacking me? I've never seen that maniac in my life before."

Scott replied, "Sandy, that maniac is Billy Smith, the guy who scared Allie and attacked Jerry. I'm very upset he attacked you like that. I think it was a case of mistaken identity. The doctor says you will need to check with him in six weeks to see if your arm is healed. You will need to keep the cast on for all that time. The wrist he's not sure about. They may have to do surgery on it as well, but for now it's in a splint."

Scott took her healthy arm and found her hand. He had tears in his eyes. Vera came and stood on the other side of Sandy's hospital bed.

"Oh, Scott, what about my work? I'll have to call in sick for the next week. I guess you won't be able to fly to Seattle now if we are short on my paycheck. Josh will be so disappointed. Oh wow, this really hurts, I'm in great pain. Where are the pain meds?"

"Don't worry about paying for the airplane ticket. I'm sure we can figure something out. I'll call Dr. Morgan, and let him know you'll not be in for the rest of this week. It's a good thing my parents are visiting here: they are very willing to stay until you get back on your feet."

Vera Brown said, "I'm so sorry this happened to you, dear. You must be in great pain. I will buzz the nurse to bring in the pain meds."

"Oh, Mother Vera. Thanks for being here for Scott and the family."

She replied, "God made sure we were here. May we pray with you?"

Sandy nodded her head and closed her eyes.

Scott prayed, "Lord Jesus, please heal Sandy up as soon as possible and give her a good night's sleep. Please take the pain away. Amen."

Vera said, "I think you'll be in the hospital for a few days while they make sure there is no infection in your arm. We'll come to visit you and have the children take turns to come and see you. Scott, why don't you give her a kiss and we can leave so she can sleep?"

"Right, we should go, Sandy."

"Wait, who saved me, was it you or Jerry?"

"Jerry saved you at the end but both Josh and I were trying to get the bat away from Billy, so he couldn't hit you again. We're happy you survived the attack, Sandy. I thank the Lord Jesus for saving you."

"I'm too tired to talk now. I can't think of anything. I need to go back to sleep. Did you buzz the nurse?"

"I'll call Dr. Morgan at home as well. He'll have to have this bad news explained to him so he can get a temp in to cover your job. When I rushed out of the house this afternoon, it was to tell you that the police found Rue Smith. They've brought her back to Spokane to stand trial for grand larceny. Also, other financial firms in other cities want to charge her with theft. We hope she will stay in jail a long time. Now they have a reason to put Billy back in custody."

Sandy mumbled, "Yes, that's wonderful news. But please leave, I need to try and rest now."

Grandma Vera prayed, "Oh Lord Jesus, we thank you for saving

Sandy's life. We pray you heal her arm and wrist as soon as possible and reduce the pain. Also, we pray she would have dreamless sleep and no nightmares. Cover her with your blood protection in this room, and may your holy angels protect her in the hospital, Lord Jesus. May the Holy Spirit bless and comfort her. Sweet sleep, Sandy. Good night."

The nurse came in and gave her pain medication. As Scott and Vera stood there beside her bed, they saw Sandy's eyes flutter and close. They tiptoed out of the room. Both Scott and his mother had tears gushing down their faces. They held hands as they went down to the parking lot, got in the car and drove back to the manse of Cornerstone Church.

His mother had told Scott that she was glad he had not revealed to Sandy that Billy Smith was in the same hospital as her. And Scott was pleased to know from the detective that Billy was in a locked room with a police officer standing guard at the door to prevent him from escaping.

When they arrived home, the whole family was sitting in the living room. Charity was in her pajamas, sitting with her Grandfather Jacob on the love seat.

"Daddy, we saved you some dinner. How's Mommy?" Charity said.

"Charity, Mommy is okay, but she had to have an operation to fix her left arm. Her left wrist is also hurt, so she'll need to stay in the hospital a few days. Your grandparents are going to stay longer to look after the family," her dad replied.

He continued, "I think everyone needs to go to bed, as it's now ten p.m. I'll just have a snack. I'm not really hungry. How about you, Mom? It's a good thing it's spring break, so everyone can sleep in tomorrow. Allie, I want you to stay home tomorrow to help your grandparents. We will need to coordinate the chores and food preparations. I'm going back to the hospital tomorrow at ten. Those of you who are ready then are welcome to join me to see your mother."

Chapter 19

Sandy woke up, wondering where she was. She noticed she was hooked up to machines and her arm was covered in a white cast. It was then she became aware of the great pain in her arm. Her wrist was aching dreadfully, too.

At that moment, a nurse came in, and said, "Oh, you're awake, Mrs. Brown. How're you feeling?"

"Awful. What time is it and what happened to me?"

"I'll get the doctor for you. It's 6 a.m. He's just starting his rounds. Dr. Webb will give you the information you want."

"I really hurt all over. When can I have some pain medication?"

"The doctor doesn't want you to get too much. You are allowed Tylenol 3s every four hours. But I can give you a top up, if you want."

Dr. Webb came through the open door of her room.

"Mrs. Brown, you're awake. How're you feeling?"

"You're my doctor? I'm in lots of pain. Why does my arm and hand hurt?"

"Yes, I'm Dr. Webb. I was your surgeon. Your left arm and wrist were broken during a fight. Your husband, Pastor Brown, will be here at ten a.m., and will fill you in on the particulars. He's the one who can explain it to you. We'll be giving you extra strong pain medication every four hours. But the nurses can give you mild top ups in between times."

"When can I go home? I want to be with my family."

The doctor continued, "In a few days, you can go home, as long as the swelling in your arm goes down. You will need to have the cast on for at least six weeks. Your wrist is also broken, but we hope immobilizing it with this splint will do the trick. You also have bruises on your face, maybe from falling out of the car."

117

"Can someone phone my husband and get him to come sooner? I want to know how this happened."

Dr Webb said, "He's not allowed here till ten a.m."

The pain receded as the drug took effect, allowing Sandy to go back to sleep. At eight, the hospital attendant brought in her breakfast tray. She helped Sandy sit up in the bed, eat her oatmeal, and gave her a cup of coffee. Twenty minutes later, the lab technician came to take some blood. The nurse returned and asked if she wanted more medication for the pain.

Sandy responded she wanted to talk to the doctor first.

The resident intern came into her room and said, "Yes, how can I help you?"

Sandy replied, "I don't remember anything. Can I have more pain medication?"

"Yes, you are allowed a top up before the four hour limit."

"Oh good. Thanks."

At ten exactly, the whole family marched towards Sandy's room. The nurse came by and put her hand up to stop them, saying only two people could go in the room at a time and to be quiet. Scott took Charity by the hand first, and brought her into her mother's room. The other relatives went to sit in the waiting room.

Rushing over to her mother's bedside, Charity said, "Wake up, Mommy! I've come to see you."

Sandy recognized her daughter's high voice and opened her eyes, "Charity, how nice to see you. Come and give me a kiss. Scott, I'm so glad to see you. I don't remember what happened. Why am I in the hospital? When can I go home?"

Charity and Scott both carefully gave Sandy a kiss on her right cheek since her left side was covered in bandages. Her right wrist had an intravenous drip in it, giving her fluids and extra pain medication. Charity started crying so Scott took her back out to the waiting room.

"Sandy, I'll come back and tell you what happened."

Going back to the waiting room he told his family that Sandy didn't remember the incident. This worried him, since he had told her the night before what had happened. But maybe the drugs were affecting her. He asked his family to pray, while he went back and told her again what happened.

When he was back in her room, he told Sandy the story once again. This time, he said she must've cut and bruised her face when she hit the car door.

"Do you remember I told you Billy Smith had attacked you? We wondered yesterday, if he mistakenly took you for Jerry from the back. Otherwise, why would he attack you like that, as you didn't even know him. Jerry does have hair as long as yours."

"Oh, that's right. I think maybe these drugs are making me woozy and forgetful."

Scott replied, "Yes. We better get the doctor to check your medication. I pray you get better really soon."

Over the next hour, each member of the family visited with Sandy in her room in pairs of two. Each time they prayed for healing for their dear mother and daughter-in-law. After they had all been in to see her, Sandy told Scott she needed to sleep now.

Scott told Sandy he would see her that night at 6:30. He needed to go into work and take everyone else back home on the way. There was no rain forecast for the next few days so his parents could keep the family occupied outside with gardening and playing basketball.

Chapter 20

Billy Smith had a huge, throbbing headache. His arm and neck were sore, too. Suddenly, he remembered some young kid had been kicking at his arm. Some other guy was trying to wrench his neck. He wasn't sure why his head hurt, especially on the right side. Billy didn't dare touch it, as it hurt too much. Or at least his head seemed to be where the main pain came from.

A male nurse came into his room. "Oh, so you're awake. That was some fight you were in. We weren't sure if you were going to make it with that huge bruise and dent on your head. It only bled a little which is amazing. Usually, head wounds bleed profusely. You can't move your arms because you are hand-cuffed to the bed. Since you started the fight and earlier had made threats, the police have you under arrest and locked to this bed."

"Who hit me? I need to know so I can hit him back."

The male nurse replied, "I don't know who hit you, but you hit a poor woman with a bat, and they thought you were going to kill her. That's why they hit you on the head."

"Well, I'm sure it's not my fault. They must've started it. How many people were there? By the way, what day and time is it? And how can I go to the restroom if I'm all locked up?"

"It's 3 p.m. on Wednesday, March 12th. You'll have to buzz me when you need to use the restroom. Here's the call button, see? A policeman is standing guard outside your room. He has the key for the handcuffs."

"I need to use the restroom, now. So, go tell the police officer to get in here with the keys, okay?"

"Hold your horses; I'm going to get him."

The male nurse opened the door and beckoned for the policeman to come inside and unlock Billy Smith's handcuffs. The nurse helped him walk to the open door of the restroom. He stood beside Billy and helped him stand up beside his intravenous pole. The policeman watched this while standing by the open hospital room door to make sure Billy didn't do anything suspicious. Since he was on an intravenous drip for pain, he wasn't able to walk very far. The nurse helped him get back into the hospital bed. Immediately, the policeman came over and locked the handcuffs to the bedrail again.

The nurse and policeman left the room and closed the door, locking it. Billy looked around the room. He saw he was alone in a small room with bars on the lone window. Beside his bed was a tray, with congealed food on it. It looked terrible. Anyway, how could he get to the meal with the cuffs on his hands? At least there was a call button he could press to get help.

He remembered he hadn't yet been able to sell all the marijuana. Billy still needed to sell two ounces. He thought he had done well to sell five ounces of the stuff in five days. Especially because the dudes he sold to said his best customers were away on holiday this week. They wouldn't be back until just before high school restarted next week.

Billy had to get out of the hospital before tomorrow. He had to sell the last of his weed before 5 p.m. Thursday. The last thing he needed was the drug dealer, Brutus, coming after him while he still had this headache. Maybe he could strike a deal with the cops? Nah, he really hated cops. They never gave him a chance.

Detective Cassidy unlocked the door and stepped into his room. "How're you doing, Billy? We have you in custody for assault and battery. You broke a woman's arm and wrist. Why did you attack her?"

"I don't remember hitting no woman. I was hitting that guy who broke my nose."

"No, you hit his poor little mother. You could have killed her, but her sons and husband came out of the house and knocked you away from her," the detective replied.

"Oh, you must be wrong. I don't hit women. They're too weak to bother with, I only like them in my bed."

"Billy, you did hit Mrs. Brown. You'll be staying in prison until your trial. There were many witnesses to the attack. Tomorrow we're planning to take you back to jail. So, get well soon."

"But wait, what about my plea bargain, if I testify against my sister? Besides, that guy hit me and gave me a headache. Why isn't he in jail?"

"Your sister is back in jail. We can't afford for you to go missing before her trial, so we were going to pick you up, anyway. But now that you have attacked another person, you're going straight to prison, with no get-out-of-jail-free card. The guy was protecting his mother from being killed so he won't be going to jail."

"That's so unfair. He's the one who should be in jail."

"Have a good evening, Billy, and sleep well."

Detective Cassidy walked out with a grin on his face, locking the door from the outside.

Billy wondered how he could escape from the hospital. A thought came to him and his face lit up in a smile. The next time the male nurse came in, he would exchange his clothes with the nurse and hurry out of the hospital. A food worker came in with his supper. He was really hungry by this time, as he was only able to reach the cold coffee with a water straw. Billy was eagerly waiting for the nurse to come in to help him eat. He was hoping they would take the cuffs off the bed railings while he ate. If he could use the restroom, he'd knock out the male nurse. How could he keep the police from locking the door on him? He would have to figure that one out soon.

Finally, at 7 p.m., a different male nurse came into the room to help Billy. He watched as at the open door of the room, there seemed to be a shift change for the policeman. It looked like no one was watching the door for a few minutes. Fortunately for Billy, this male nurse was large and muscular and looked the right size to switch clothes with him.

"Hello, Billy. Are you getting hungry? It looks like it's hard for you to eat with those cuffs on your hands. The policemen are just changing shifts, so he gave me the key to unlock the cuffs. This way, you can eat your dinner easily."

"What's your name? I can't read the name plate from here," replied Billy as he tried to get the nurse closer to him.

"Do you need glasses? My name is Chad, like the movie star." At this point he took off Billy's gown and helped him get into another one with no blood on it. The nurse also made him turn on his side so Billy could have a clean sheet under him.

Billy grimaced and said, "I don't know any movie star with that name. Oh, thanks for getting the cuffs off. They're really rubbing the skin on my arms. Plus, I have these big bruises on my right arm. Well, what do you know, this roast beef, gravy and potatoes tastes just fine. It's better than my lunch."

Nurse Chad replied, "Well, what did you have for lunch, Billy?"

While the nurse was talking, Billy shoveled the food into his mouth as fast as he could. He wanted to be ready for anything. As he was eating, he mumbled through his teeth, "I didn't have anything for lunch, because it was cold and awful looking by the time I woke up. Besides, they had the cuffs on me so I couldn't reach the food."

"Okay, since you've finished your dinner so quickly, do you need help walking to the restroom?"

"Yeah, that would be great. If you can help me out of bed and let me lean my left side on your arm, I'll be able to walk," Billy replied.

The male nurse unhooked Billy's arm from the IV stand but the drip for pain was left in his arm. As he was walking towards the restroom, Billy wondered what he could use to knock Chad out.

Standing there at the toilet, he quickly finished and grabbed a cane that was standing in the corner of the restroom behind the door.

Just as the nurse came to ask him if he needed any more help, Billy hiding the cane behind his back said, "Can you get me a blanket? I feel so cold here."

As the nurse turned around, Billy clobbered him on the back of the head with the cane. He was hit so hard he didn't make a sound as he fell to the floor. As quickly as he could, Billy pulled off the male nurse's trousers and put them on himself. He unbuttoned the man's shirt, and took it off. Removing his hospital gown, Billy put on the male nurse's uniform. He looked in the cupboard and found his socks, shoes and his wallet.

The male nurse was lying silently on the ground in Billy's hospital room. He tiptoed to the door, and carefully opened it a crack. The police guard was not there. Oh boy, how great, he was free.

He saw a nurse coming down the hall, so he quickly walked through the door, turning away, and locking it from the outside. Billy used a clipboard to hide the bruises on his arm. He covered his cuts by wearing a surgical mask and a head covering. Billy walked slowly down the 6th floor exit stairs, trying not to wince from his headache.

He couldn't believe his luck. Billy looked out the ground floor exit door, seeing no cops looking for him. But he heard yelling, so he quickly moved out the door and turned the other way. It was a bit hard to run with his headache, but he needed to get back to his stash of drugs and change of clothes. Luckily, the hospital was only about six blocks from his hideout in the forest near the high school.

When he got there, Billy carefully looked around. He was glad that school was not in session so nobody could see him. He quickly dug up his drug stash and backpack with his extra pair of clothes in it. If he did say it himself, he looked really good wearing his new clothes. He even had a beret to wear, so people wouldn't be able to spot his blood and bruises. Billy really liked his fake leather jacket which covered up the rest of his bruises.

When he came back later that night, he had sold the last two ounces of the pot. He had decided he needed more money so he had charged double the price per baggie. Brutus would never know. He still had a small pinch left. However, Billy's head was starting to hurt terribly, so he thought he would spend $40 on a motel and get some rest.

When he woke up, he saw it was already 4 p.m. the next afternoon. He couldn't believe it. Soon it would be 5. Well, he would tell Brutus someone had stolen the last two ounces from him and he would just have to owe him the money cause he needed to get some money out of the sale too. He got up and moved as quickly as he could down the road.

Precisely at 5 p.m., Brutus turned up near the forest where he said he would be. He looked around and noticed Yak limping slowly towards him. He didn't look in very good shape.

"What happened to you, Yak? You're late. I don't like having to wait for anyone," Brutus complained.

"Hold on, I'm here. I have your money except the last $100. Some of those black dudes stole my last pound of weed so I will have to owe you. I have $640 for you. I was in the hospital yesterday because they beat me up."

"Do you remember what I told you? If you didn't bring me all of the money, you'd regret it. Remember you owe me an extra $70? Can I run a business if you cheat me? Tommy and Paul, come here," Brutus yelled.

Suddenly two very large white guys charged at Billy out of the forest and started beating him. Quickly, Brutus walked away from the beating. Tommy and Paul hit him so many times on his head that Billy fell down unconscious. After taking his wallet and last $20, the thugs walked away nonchalantly, as they believed no one had seen them. They left Billy on the ground, all bloody and dirty, in the middle of the forest.

The police had been looking for Billy since the night before. The nurse, Chad, to whom Billy had given a severe brain injury, was put into a coma to try to save his life. No one knew if he would survive or not.

Detective Cassidy had just got a tip from the owner of a motel who listened to the police reports. He said he recognized Billy from their description as a person who had rented a motel room from him for two nights. Maybe he was there right now, as he hadn't seen him leave.

The police swiftly drove over there without sirens as they neared the motel. They wanted to surprise him. Detective Cassidy yelled, "Police!" and they broke down the door. Much to their surprise, he wasn't there. All his possessions still appeared to be there, including Nurse Chad's uniform in the garbage. Cassidy was pleased to see that Billy had hidden some marijuana under the mattress wrapped in two one-hundred-dollar bills. Now the police could charge him with possession, drug trafficking, assault, and attempted murder. Billy Smith would not be out of prison for a long time.

Since Billy had obviously been selling drugs, Detective Cassidy went with some undercover officers to the Red Pool Hall on Center Street. He waited outside while the undercover officers talked to some of the teens. They all said Billy usually hung out by Whitmore High School. The police raced over there with sirens blaring.

No one was near the school. But over in the forest, it looked like there had been a fight. There were broken branches and leaves all over the place. A police officer yelled at Detective Cassidy and waved his hand for him to come over.

"Sir, we found him. He's in very poor shape. You need to call the ambulance. I don't think he's going to make it."

Detective Cassidy went over to look. There was Billy Smith on his back with his face covered in bruises. He was wearing new clothes that were now covered in blood. The detective bent down to feel for a pulse. There was none. He pulled Billy's eyelid up, and saw no response from his pupil.

"Yeah, I think you're right," said Detective Cassidy. "He's gone. But we still have to call an ambulance, and get a doctor to certify he's dead. Call 911. We need the homicide detectives here. Don't touch anything and stay away from the crime scene."

Cassidy thought to himself if Billy was dead, that could solve a few problems for the Brown family. He wouldn't need to charge Billy with murder either, if Nurse Chad Martin didn't make it. The ambulance turned up, and the paramedics examined the body. The paramedics agreed Billy Smith was dead, but they would get a doctor to confirm it. Now he was dead, the police would have to wait for the coroner to come and check out the body. It was going to be a long night.

Chapter 21

Sandy had been able to come home three days earlier. But it was painful for her to have to sit and do nothing. The astounding news was that Billy Smith, after escaping from the hospital, was found dead near Whitmore High School. Someone, other than Jerry, had hit him on the head several times. Apparently, he had bruises all over his face, as well. With his sister Rue Smith in jail, Sandy wondered who would go to Billy's funeral or even if he would have a funeral. She felt bad about this, but she was glad he was dead. He had terrorized her family. She still had nightmares about being attacked. It made her so angry at the guy even though he was dead. How could she ever have closure when she couldn't even face him and give him an impact statement? The emotional and physical damage he had inflicted on her was terrible. Even though he was dead, she still didn't feel like forgiving him. She didn't know if she ever could. Her husband encouraged her to, but she just couldn't.

Because Sandy was injured, Scott's parents had agreed to stay another week. Thank God. Since they were staying longer, they would drive Scott to Seattle for Josh's race in the beginning of April. Sandy was beginning to feel better and could move around, so Scott decided he could go to Josh's race. He now only had to pay for a one-way ticket on the evening flight back to Spokane, and his parents had agreed to cover the cost for that. They were all thankful that their other teens were receiving counselling.

Allie was so happy she didn't have to be looking over her shoulder every day. She hated the guy and wanted to beat his brains out, but now she couldn't. Last week, her counselor, Kerry, had said she would feel freer if she became willing to forgive him. But she wasn't ready.

Allie said to her counselor, "How can I forgive him when he's dead? I can't get him to say he's sorry. Besides, it was never likely he would apologize for harassing me and talking dirty to me. He was so creepy. It still makes me feel dirty he tried to touch me."

Kerry the counselor responded, "I'm sorry to hear this. Thank God he's no longer around to harass you. Often, I have found that if we pray, it can help you feel better. Let me know if you want us to pray together."

Allie stood up, turned away, and walked over to the window, saying, "I'm not ready to forgive him, so I don't think I'm ready to have prayers. Thanks, anyway."

Kerry came to stand beside Allie, and said quietly, "I understand. Forgiveness takes time. It is for your own sake, Allie. In the Bible in Matthew 18, Jesus tells a parable about the first servant who asked the king to forgive his huge debt. The king gave the servant mercy. But since the first servant didn't forgive his fellow servant, neither would the king forgive him. Jesus said you put yourself in jail and become chained to that person if you don't forgive them. The Lord says you need to forgive your brother or sister, seventy times seven times, daily. Otherwise God can't forgive you."

Allie twisted around to stare at her, "But Kerry, the guy's dead now, so I can't forgive him. Anyway, my dad says you aren't supposed to speak to the dead."

Kerry nodded her head in agreement and said, "Pastor Brown is correct. Once people are dead, it's up to Jesus to deal with them. If you want Jesus Christ to help you to deal with this, ask Him to help you forgive Billy. Jesus can be trusted to deal with him. It'll make you feel better inside. Why not pray? Tell the Lord Jesus you can't do it by yourself. You could ask Him to help you choose to forgive Billy Smith from your will."

"I might consider that, Kerry. I'll have to think about it."

Looking carefully at Allie, Kerry replied, "There are probably people who are still living now that you need to forgive, not just Billy Smith. What if you wrote down anyone you need to forgive and then ask the

Lord Jesus to help you? It might be easier to start with members of your family rather than Billy Smith."

Allie glanced back at Kerry, while continuously moving her leg back and forth, "Do you mean you want me to do all this on my own before next week?"

"Well, Allie, that's up to you. I know you would feel freer inside if you could work on forgiving friends and family. Sometimes I have to forgive my husband daily for little things that bug me. There might be family members or friends you need to forgive, too. See you next week at the same time."

Jerry didn't know if he wanted to see the counselor today. Everything was so strange now. Jerry couldn't really believe Billy Smith was dead. He was extremely relieved. When he heard Billy had escaped from the hospital prison room, he'd been afraid to leave his house, again. Jerry had not intended to kill Billy, but after he hit him on the head, he was fearful he had. He was very angry at that guy for hurting his mother. It was good his grandparents were paying the cost of him coming to see the same counselor as Allie. Having someone he could trust to tell his thoughts to and not blab his secrets to anyone was a big relief.

Kerry said, "Hi Jerry, come on in. Would you like a fruit drink, water, or tea?

"Kerry, may I have a drink of orange juice, please?"

Handing him the cup of juice, she said, "Okay, here's your drink. Jerry, how're you doing today?

Sitting back on the couch, he responded, "Kerry, I'm stoked I don't have to worry about that guy anymore. It's too bad he got murdered, but he was a maniac. I feel really angry at God. If he loves me so much, why did he put me in danger? It happened to me twice. TWICE." Jerry banged his fist on the couch.

Looking carefully at him, she said, "Knowing this assailant can't come after you again, must be a big relief. It seems to me God protected you twice now. Jerry, God really loves you."

Then he whispered, "That's hard to accept. I could've been dead. He was one crazy dude. I don't know how I survived him." And he jumped up and started pacing the floor.

Kerry paused and said, "It's good you feel angry. That means you're not frozen any more. Do you remember when you came in here two months ago? You wouldn't even talk to me. Okay, now where is the anger?... Do you know that anger is often the mind's way to cover for fear?"

Jerry collapsed again into his chair and started flinging his hands in the air as he yelled, "Kerry, I'm not afraid. I'm angry. I feel angry all the time right here in my abdomen."

He pointed to his stomach. "I have a big ball of fire in there which hurts so much. I've been having trouble eating and sleeping since the big fight with that dude. I feel guilty for hitting him with the poker. I thought I killed the guy. What a relief he didn't die from that hit."

Kerry nodded her head replying, "I'm glad he didn't die too, you have enough on your plate."

Jerry looked down at the floor and admitted with a little laugh, "Now the only thing I can keep down is vanilla ice cream and brown rice but not at the same time. I'm worried I might start losing weight. I only weigh 135 pounds, at six feet. Kerry, I don't want to disappear."

Kerry looked sad and replied, "Jerry, you won't disappear. Can you take a big breath and let it out, slowly? That should help make your gut feel better. Do it again. ... Big sigh. Just help yourself calm down. That's it. If you do this daily, you'll start feeling better inside. I pray you'll get your appetite back. How is your thinking?"

Jerry slumped down in his chair, "I don't know but sometimes I wonder what's the point? It's been hard to be happy. I feel down most of the time. I can't believe all the things that have happened to me. First, there were good things and now only the bad things."

Sitting right back in her chair, Kerry nodded her head and said, "I understand. It's been really tough for you. I'm believing you will see a shift for the better. It was wonderful you won the award for your song and had your close friend, Samantha, help you."

She continued, "But it's horrible you were attacked by Billy twice. God must have sent his holy angels to protect you. I think it's a miracle you were not permanently maimed or even killed. And the second time, you saved your mother's life. Good on you, you're a hero, Jerry."

Jerry shook his head and looked out the window and whispered, "I don't feel like a hero, Kerry. Come on, I'm only 15 years old. It hurts me to see my mom with a broken arm when it was supposed to be me. I'm afraid to go to bed at night as I have nightmares about this fight. Now that it's spring break at least I can sleep in."

Kerry replied, "I'm sorry for you. It sounds painful. Did you know that there are psalms in the Bible that can help you sleep?"

Getting out her bible, she continued, "Psalm 3 says: 'You are a shield around me. I lie down and sleep; I wake again because the Lord sustains me. I'll not fear though tens of thousands assail me on every side.' Psalm 4 says: 'I will lie down and sleep for you alone, Lord, make me dwell in safety.'

Standing up she gave Jerry these passages from the bible and said, "Jerry, here are these psalms for you to read for yourself. Or you could get your parents to read them over you, before you fall asleep at night. What do you think?"

Jerry threw his legs out from the chair and stood up, "Maybe. Let me think about telling my parents. It's private."

Kerry turned and shook his hand, "Okay, I'll leave it with you to decide."

She let go of his hand and asked, "Can I pray for you now, Jerry?" He nodded his head yes and sat back down in his chair.

She said, "Lord Jesus, I pray Jerry can let the anger and fear go out of his life. May he sense how much you love him. Help him to know you have his back and will keep him safe."

Jerry sighed and smiled at his counselor, "That makes me feel a little better. I know I need something to help me sleep, maybe some medication? Usually I play my guitar for a long time which makes me so tired I fall asleep. But I haven't felt like playing my guitar since my mom got attacked."

Kerry responded, "I'm reluctant to recommend medication too quickly. Let's try prayer and reading the Bible first before I call Dr. Morgan about this. Do you have any physical pain? Let me know, please. I want to see you again, tomorrow at ten. Will that work?"

Jerry touched his sore hand saying, "Yes, my pinkie finger still hurts from being cut. I'm thinking I need to get it checked by the doctor in case I have an infection from the stitches. And yeah, I'm free tomorrow at ten so I can make it."

"Good, I'll put you in my book for then. Please get checked out at the doctor's office." She got out of her chair and took him to the door.

"Kerry, remember I told you I won an award and a chance to have my song *Peace for You* played on the radio station? So, all this week at 4 p.m., they've been playing my song. It's great, but I don't feel peace. The song doesn't do it for me anymore."

Kerry replied, "Wow, this is really great. A local radio station's playing your song? I'll make a note of this and tune into the station at 4 this afternoon."

Standing just inside the door, he said, "But Kerry I don't feel great. I don't even want to see any of my friends. All they want to talk about is my fights with that loser. It brings back all the bad memories. Thank God, I have my brother Josh to shoot hoops with me. Since he was also in the last fight, he gets that I don't want to talk about it. He's a great kid brother."

"I'm sad to hear you don't want to play guitar, or see your friends, Jerry. Can I pray for you again, as our session is ending?"

Jerry stood still replying, "I guess so."

"Dear Lord Jesus, I know you love Jerry very much. Lord, I pray he can sense your peace in his heart. We both agree Jerry would like to be able to sleep soundly again. Lord Jesus, may he know your peace this night and have no more nightmares.

She smiled at him, saying, "Jerry, please think about talking to your parents about praying Psalm three and four over you. I'll be praying for you. It takes time to get over a big trauma like this. See you tomorrow."

Jerry nodded his head and left the room. Allie was waiting for him in the waiting room. She'd been praying and crying for him while he was in his session. She had just realized how much trauma he'd gone through in a few weeks. It was horrible what had happened to him. Plus, it reminded her of all the people she needed to forgive, including Jerry. As Allie was wiping her eyes with the back of her hand, Jerry came up to her and gave her a hug. Together in solidarity, they walked the ten blocks home.

After a while, Allie said, "Did you know there's this woman in Rwanda who forgave the man who killed her husband and son? Kerry was telling me about it. Did you know it's a true story? He was in prison there and some evangelists came to the prison and he gave his heart to the Lord Jesus. When he came back to the same village, the woman who had been his neighbor wasn't happy. She was still afraid of him and hated him. In her heart she wanted to kill him in revenge, but of course she didn't do that. Instead they were put together into the same reconciliation group in the village. She couldn't believe it when he acted remorseful. He even volunteered to rebuild her house that had been destroyed. But he did, and now they're friends. This is called restitution. Now she has forgiven him. Isn't that amazing?"

Jerry stopped, turned to her and said, "It sounds like a fairy tale to me. Why would she forgive him for destroying her family? I couldn't do that."

Allie replied, "All I know is the woman in Rwanda did. We need to learn to stick together as family. I know, Jerry, you've had a really hard time these last few months. We need to pray we can all get over this. I have trouble sleeping sometimes. How about you?"

He nodded his head. "Yeah, I have trouble sleeping most nights. I'm not sure what to do about it."

"Jer, I wonder how the rest of the family are doing. I'll have to have a talk with Mom."

"Allie, I think Mom is really struggling. Dad and Josh seem okay to me. But of course, both you and I know we have our issues. Allie, do we have to talk about this? Let's not, okay? Have you listened to my song *'Peace for You'* on the radio? It sounds great, right?"

"It's totally awesome. Yeah, Jerry, I've been listening every day. That's so great your song is on the radio."

"Thanks, Allie."

Allie added, "By the way, do you think they're going to have a funeral for Billy? Who would even want to go to that guy's funeral? His only relative is Rue Smith, and she's in jail."

Jerry stopped, raised his healthy hand up and said, "I don't want to hear that name, again. How's your boyfriend doing? Are you going out to a movie this week? I heard *Free Willy 2* is playing at the movie theater. I sure wish I could take Samantha to a movie."

Allie looked surprised. She felt compassion for her brother as they continued to walk along the road.

"Maybe, Dad and Mom would let you go on a group date to the movie theater with us. I'll ask whether that could be a possibility when we get home."

"Sweet. Thanks, Allie. I think my friends would like to go as a group to celebrate my song making it on the radio. Awesome."

Jerry ran up to his room while Allie walked deliberately into the living room to see her mother. She sat in a chair directly across from her. On the couch, her mother sat with her arm in the cast. There were several pillows supporting it while she read her Bible. Allie saw her grimace but when she looked up, Sandy smiled at her daughter.

"How's the pain, Mom? "

"Today the pain in my arm isn't too bad. My wrist throbs all the time but the medication helps."

Allie responded, "I'm glad it's feeling better. It has been almost a week. It's spring break, so I was wondering if Jerry could come with Lewis and me to the movies, tomorrow night at seven? We were also thinking it would be nice if Jerry could invite his music friends, including Samantha, to the new *Free Willy 2* movie. I know you don't want Jerry to date, but this would be a group event, not a date. What do you think?"

"It might be possible. Tell me more."

"Jerry hasn't had any fun since spring break started. This would give him something positive to think about. We agreed it could be a celebration of his song being played on the radio. After the movie, we could go out for pizza. Tomorrow is the last day of our vacation. Please say yes. Dad could pick us all up at ten p.m. if you aren't going anywhere." Allie smiled at her mom and put her arm around her.

Sandy smiled, saying, "Allie, I see you have this all figured out. Dad and I are not opposed to a group event. If you and Jerry can get it organized, I think Dad will agree. I know Jerry's had it rough this week, again. It was supposed to be relaxing, being off school. Who expected to be attacked by Billy Smith twice in two months?"

Allie nodded her head. "I know, it's hard to take it all in."

Sandy continued, "I hate the guy for what he did but at least he's dead now. You know, Allie, in the Bible it says to forgive people but I'm really having trouble with that. Every time I have an ache, I remember what that guy did to me. Wow, I never knew forgiving was so hard."

"Mom, our counselor says you need to forgive your enemies, so you won't be chained to them. I know it's hard to forgive that guy for all he did, but I'm trying to get up the courage to try."

"I know all the scriptures, Allie, but it's different when you're the one in pain. This guy broke my arm and wrist, and I can't work for at least another week. I ache everywhere. It may take me a long time to forgive this man if ever. I think maybe I will have to go to your counselor, as well, and talk it out with her."

"Mom, that would be a good idea, she's really helpful."

Chapter 22

Scott Brown was having trouble concentrating on his sermon. He kept getting flashbacks of the fight with Billy Smith. He'd better book an appointment with the counselor for himself. Maybe she would have some insight on how to get rid of these bad memories. He felt guilty he had attacked Billy Smith, especially now he was dead.

Scott had thought he would have a chance to talk with Billy. He had also hoped to give a victim impact statement at his trial to help deal with the aftermath of the big fight. Sandy was still in plenty of pain, and not dealing well with the emotional trauma of being attacked. He still didn't understand how that creep could think she was Jerry. The attacker must have been in a blind rage and seeing someone with the same coloring as Jerry had assumed it was him.

He was surprised Billy had discovered where they lived. But Detective Cassidy was sure he had been following Jerry for a few days, looking for an opportunity to attack him again. Scott was sure making Jerry and Allie have someone with them at all times had saved their lives.

Scott would phone Debra and ask her to pray for him, as he wasn't getting anything done today at the church office.

"Hello Debra, I'm having trouble concentrating on my sermon, because of the incident which happened last Saturday. Would you pray for me, please?"

"Pastor Scott, why don't you have Dan Jordan, the youth pastor, preach this Sunday? It's spring break and most of the teens are away, so give yourself a break, too."

"Well, that's a possibility, Debra. Let me think about it. Thanks."

"Okay, let's pray. Dear Jesus, we pray Pastor Scott will be able to concentrate on finishing his sermon. But we also pray he would accept influence and allow someone else to preach this Sunday, if it's your will."

"Thanks for praying. I've another idea about who can preach, as Dan needs a break, too. But I'll let you know as soon as I know. Thanks for the suggestion to have a day off this Sunday from preaching. Funny, last week I was fine, but it has started to hit me hard now with flashbacks."

When Scott returned home, he saw Josh and Jerry playing one on one basketball on the front driveway. It looked like they were evenly matched. Both of his sons were making the basket every time. They looked happy.

Scott came into the living room and sat down on the couch with Sandy. "Dear. Do you know where my dad is? I'm going to ask him if he would preach this Sunday. My head feels cloudy, and no thoughts or ideas are coming for my sermon. Do you think it's a good idea to take this Sunday off?"

"Hi, honey. Your dad's downstairs in his room, I think. He's probably taking a nap. You know, that's a really good idea to get someone else to preach this week. Maybe we should all stay home and take a break. I hope your dad will be willing to preach for you."

"I think he will. But I don't think it's a good idea for everyone to stay home. I understand you're not able, and maybe Jerry, but the rest of us should go. Everyone at church is looking forward to seeing my parents again."

"Well, okay, but Jerry might want to go to church, too. Don't ask him, just assume he will go and hope he does."

He carefully touched her healthy right arm and gave her a grin.

Sandy continued, "Allie has gone to the mall with Lewis and Sue. She asked me if Jerry might go to the movie with her and her friends, tomorrow. But she also asked that if it was a group event, could Jerry bring his friends, including Samantha. I thought a group event would be fine, but I said I would check with you. It's the new movie *Free Willy 2*. Jerry could use a distraction. She suggested it could be a celebration time for him for the success of his song being played on KKZX radio. So, what do you think? I thought that you might pick them all up in the van, after they go out for pizza."

Scott took her right hand and replied, "Well, it sounds like you and Allie have it all organized. What time is the movie? I think a group event is okay, as long as Jerry is not alone with Samantha. Has he seen her or any of his other friends since the incident last Saturday?"

She responded, "No, I haven't seen any of them around. He just seems to sit in his room in silence or plays hoops with Josh. If they go tomorrow the movie starts at 7 p.m. The pizza place is just down the street from the movie theater. Is that okay with you? Scott, you could pick them up from there at ten p.m. in our van."

"Yes, I will pick them up tomorrow after their pizza. After I go down and speak to my dad, I think I'll go up and have a snooze. Did you get a nap today? They say extra sleep actually helps you heal. I need to talk to the detective about funeral plans for Billy Smith. I feel bad there seems to be no one except his sister to mourn for him."

After getting his dad to agree to preaching on the next Sunday Scott went into his office and closed the door. He looked up the detective's direct phone number at work and called him.

"Hello, Detective Cassidy? This is Pastor Scott Brown. I was wondering if there are any funeral plans for Billy Smith?"

"Hi, Pastor. Yes, Rue Smith has demanded they have a funeral for Billy Smith at the Roman Catholic Church. She says her grandmother and mother were both devout Roman Catholics. The funeral Mass will be on Monday after they have finished the autopsy for Billy Smith."

"Oh, thanks for letting me know. I want to be at the funeral, in case I can offer any help to her."

"Well, I doubt she'll want your help. But if you like, I could ask if she will agree to see you."

The next day at 5 p.m., Allie, Lewis, Sue, Jim, and Jerry met Samantha at the bus stop so they could go to *Free Willy 2* together. Cassie and Luke were going to meet them at the movie theater at 6:50. Everyone was excited to be together and see the movie. They bought their tickets, popcorn, candy and drinks and went to sit in the fourth row of the theater.

Cassie made sure to sit beside Jim, who sat beside Jerry, who was sitting with Samantha. On Samantha's other side were Allie, Lewis, Sue and finally Luke. Allie was surprised Luke was there. She didn't know

Sue even knew him. He was a friend of Lewis' and was a really good basketball player. Luke was as tall as him, so that was probably part of the attraction for Sue. It was rare for a guy to be taller than she was.

Jerry was pleased Jim had brought a friend with him. He didn't know Cassie liked Jim or that she was his friend. He was thrilled Samantha was sitting right beside him, her leg touching his leg, while holding on to his healthy hand as he offered her popcorn with the other one.

Allie was delighted to be sitting beside Lewis with his arm around her. She was beginning to think she loved him. She could see herself marrying him once they both graduated from college. His blue eyes were so dreamy and always looked so kindly at her. It was a great movie and everyone enjoyed being there and eating the pizza afterwards. They had great night after all the trauma the Brown teens had had in their lives recently.

Chapter 23

Rue Smith was sick and tired of being in a prison cell. For a few days, she could handle it. But now she wanted out. Her cellmate, Kim, was okay, but she wasn't very smart. She'd been picked up for soliciting and it wasn't for the first time. Rue found this sad and tried to encourage her to get her GED diploma so she could get a better job.

Rue never had any real girlfriends. So, it was fun and helped with the boredom to tell Kim all about her escapades. She told Kim that she actually had money hidden in the Cayman Islands. She even invited Kim to come and visit her there if she ever got out of jail. Rue was sure she would get out soon, since her brother was now dead and there was no one to testify against her. The little brat had ratted her out, and claimed that Rue had stolen the computers and files. She laughed and bragged to Kim that no one knew how much she had really stolen. The authorities would never find her stash as it was registered under a different name in the Cayman Islands. She had several million dollars stowed there. It gave her great joy she had saved this money. The undercover police officer Kim who was sharing the cell with Rue was also pleased with this nugget of information.

Billy didn't have any idea how much Rue had really stolen. That's what happens when you're not a blood relative, just a half brother. It was good she hadn't trusted him. He was a stool pigeon. She now had five million dollars sitting in a bank in the Cayman Islands under the name of Jackie Harris.

What good memories she had from those warm islands. In the Caribbean, Rue Smith had met and dated many handsome men who were also scammers like her. In fact, this was why she had had to return suddenly to the United States. She was very annoyed that someone whom she had trusted had tricked her into gambling away $50,000 of her hard-earned loot. It was while Pierre was swindling rich Americans with fake Caribbean real estate. Somehow, the authorities had discovered what he was doing. Rue didn't want to be caught in the fallout and scrambled back to her hiding place in Boise, Idaho. She wasn't sure how the police had figured out where she was in Idaho. Someday she would find out who had tattled on her.

She heard a guard yelling her name. Really, it was about time. She'd been waiting for an hour for this interview.

"Smith, you are wanted by Detective Cassidy in the visitors' room. Come with me right now. Hurry up."

Opening the locked cell, he brought her out, keeping her handcuffs and shackles snug on her body. Every once in a while, the guard would push her in the back with his baton, telling her to get moving. Ten minutes later, she was sitting at the table with Detective Cassidy. The prison guard had refused to remove her shackles and handcuffs, even though Cassidy was already there. The detective stared at the guard, motioning for him to take the restraints off. The guard glared back at Detective Cassidy but reluctantly did as he was ordered.

Cassidy said, "Nice to see you, Rue. When you are guarded in the jail you are allowed to have the chains off while I interview you. Have they been treating you well?"

"Well, detective, what do you think? I want out of here immediately; do you hear me? Where's my court-appointed lawyer? I want to hire a real lawyer. My brother's dead and you have no other witnesses to testify against me."

"I offer my condolences on the death of your brother. But we can't let you out because we have other witnesses besides your brother. We can phone the public defender's office and get you a lawyer from there as you don't seem to have any money. Also, we videotaped his confession before he left the jail and got himself murdered. By the way, the funeral is set for next Monday at two in the afternoon at the Holy Rosary Cathedral. For the funeral, you will be permitted to wear your own clothes. You'll also temporarily be allowed to be free of the shackles. Do you want to say a few words at his funeral Mass?"

"I don't believe you have any other witnesses and I don't think you can use the recording of a dead person as a witness. Get me a real lawyer. I know my rights. Of course, I'll speak at Billy's funeral Mass. We didn't have the best relationship as a family but I did love him. Unfortunately, our father beat Billy as a little kid. So, that was the only way he was taught to relate to other people. He was hit on the head many times when he was little, I think the abuse made it hard for him to concentrate in school, too.

"We stayed with our grandparents after that because we were afraid our father would kill us one day. Billy didn't have any friends once we moved. We'd left all our friends back in Portland, Oregon. My grandfather would go into rages at any noise the little guy would make and he beat Billy on the shoulders and buttocks many times. We were both so happy when my grandfather died. I'll be glad to get up and do a talk for my poor misguided brother who never made it past tenth grade. He was only a half brother so my mom and grandma didn't want him. I wish he had stayed in Oregon. Maybe he'd have been okay there. We did have one kind aunt who lived in Portland, Oregon. But my mother was jealous of Aunt Tracy and wouldn't let us stay with her."

Detective Cassidy replied, "Well, I'm shocked Billy's dead. I was looking forward to charging him for all the robberies and assaults he had committed in the last few months. It was quite the crime spree. We've not been able to figure out yet who killed him. I know it wasn't the Browns because they were all trying to keep away from him. Plus, they all have alibis."

"I hate those Browns," said Rue. "Isn't Pastor Brown Vicki Broadmoor's preacher? I bet he was trying to keep Jake from leaving town with me. They were the ones who attacked poor Billy. He was only trying to get revenge on that nasty Jerry Brown since he broke Billy's nose."

"Well, no one else thought it was fair that Billy attacked Mrs. Brown. On another topic, do you know who Billy's enemies might be? We did find some money and drugs hidden at the motel where he was staying. Did you know if he was on drugs?"

"I never saw him take any drugs. He liked to drink beer, but that was it. Our mother died of a drug overdose, so we vowed we would stay away from drugs. Plus, our father was beaten to death by his drug dealer for cheating him out of $50. I wonder if Billy had money and drugs because he was selling for a drug dealer. I know a guy called Brutus. He tried to get me to be his babe but I refused. I hear he uses dudes like Billy to sell his drugs for him. Why don't you try and find him? Maybe he killed Billy. There, I've just solved the crime for you. I'd sure like to have you find whoever did this to my poor brother. Nobody deserves to die even if they weren't very smart."

Rue smiled at Detective Cassidy, then frowned as the prison guard leered at her.

"Okay, Rue, it's time for you to go back to your cell," said Detective Cassidy.

"Hey, wait. Detective Cassidy, when is my lawyer coming to see me? I'm sure you don't have a case now."

Rue looked at the detective pleadingly, and unsuccessfully tried to move away to prevent having the restraints put back on. The prison guard was very happy to manhandle her. The shackles and cuffs went back on her arms and legs. She stood up with a resigned look on her face.

As he began to stand up, the detective replied, "We know about your other scams as well, Rue. The other businessmen are willing to testify at your trial. It wasn't only Jake Broadmoor that lost money or confidential work files to you. As I said I will phone the public defender's office and try and get one to come and see you today."

She looked worried as the guard pushed her out the door with his baton and down the corridor to her cell. How could she ever escape from prison? She smiled to herself. When she made it back to her cell, she laughed aloud as her idea was simply outrageous.

Chapter 24

Jake was pleased they had found Rue Smith and she had been brought back to Spokane to stand trial. But he was a bit concerned now that Billy was dead. Who else did they have to testify that she had stolen all the money and files? Dr. Morgan could verify that she had drugged Jake, so at least there was proof of that. He still was astounded he had fallen for her smooth flattering voice. What a deceptive woman she was.

Things were not yet good with Vicki, but it was great to be seeing his little boys once again. His mother Debra was a solid, kind mother and grandmother. His sisters still didn't want to have anything to do with him. Maybe they would come around, if Vicki would agree to see him. Debra said Vicki was doing well and was enjoying her part-time job at the coffee shop two blocks over from her house. She could walk to work from home while Debra looked after the grandchildren.

It was terrible to hear what had happened to the Brown family. Thank God, no one else had been killed. Billy Smith had been horrible, the vicious way he had attacked Sandy Brown. Jake was beginning to see Pastor Scott's point of view. It was better to forgive Rue and Billy, rather than have them always on your mind. He hoped he could start to forgive them. Since God had forgiven his sins, he was beginning to see maybe he could forgive Rue her sins against him.

Pastor Brown said forgiveness didn't mean you forgot what the person did. You were allowed to have boundaries, and weren't required to be good friends with people who had hurt you. It would be easier to forgive Rue and Billy if he could get some more of his firm's money back. Jake was trying to forgive his wife, Vicki, for her refusal to see

him. It still hurt. He would always love her, though he'd messed up so dreadfully.

Detective Ewart from the Homicide Department was delighted to hear from Detective Cassidy about Rue Smith's tip. It might have been Brutus the drug dealer or one of his gang who had killed Billy. He knew it couldn't be Pastor Brown, as he had an alibi, and appeared very truthful. Nobody had a bad thing to say about the entire family.

He would tell his partner, Jodie Kline. They would get some undercover cops to talk to their informants about Brutus.

His phone rang. Picking it up, he responded, "Yes, this is Detective Ewart. You have some information on the Billy Smith homicide? Okay, I will tell my partner, and we will be outside the pool hall in twenty minutes. Wait there, and we will pick you up. We'll talk to you at the picnic area in the park."

Detective Ewart looked at his partner Jodie and said, "Kline, it looks like we have a breakthrough in the Billy Smith case. Let's go."

As they were driving to the pool hall, Detective Kline remarked, "Wouldn't it be great if we could get Brutus off the street? You know, I think he has killed before, but we never had any proof. I hope our informant is solid."

Arriving at the pool hall, they noticed a teen with light blonde hair waiting for them. Detective Ewart drove up beside her, and the girl got in the car.

"Hello, I'm Detective Kline. What's your name? Thanks for speaking to us," Detective Kline said.

The park was empty at the moment as it was dinner time so the detectives hoped they would not be interrupted. They all went to sit at a picnic table beside the children's playground

"My name is Sue Montgomery. During spring break, I was working at the Gap. I always take a short cut across the park after school or work. The day of the murder, I was coming home, and heard all this shouting and grunting. I looked towards the forest and saw Brutus walking away, while two of his thugs were beating this guy up. I didn't want to get caught by them. So, I ran behind the school, and down the alley to my house. I have never run so fast in my life."

"Are you sure it was Brutus? What did he look like?" asked Detective Ewart.

"Well, it sure looked like him. I've seen Brutus hanging around the school and the pool hall. He has a scruffy yellow beard and limp blonde hair. This guy was wearing a grey hoodie and blue jeans. He also had sunglasses on so I think it was him as he always wears shades. Because he's known to be dangerous, I didn't want to get too close to see if it was Brutus."

Detective Kline agreed, "It does sound like his description. He may not have committed the murder but he could be charged with conspiracy to commit murder. What did the two other guys look like?"

Sue answered, "I couldn't really see them clearly through the trees, but both were big and blond haired. I didn't see their faces. I mostly heard them swearing at the guy they were beating up. I might be able to recognize their voices. The one guy had a low raspy voice with a lisp. The other one had a really high voice like a little girl."

Detective Ewart said, "Thanks for your description. We will check with our informants and try to find these guys. Don't tell anyone that you talked to us because you don't want it getting back to Brutus. You know he is very volatile and cruel."

"Okay, thanks for believing me. My mom didn't even want to hear about it. I told my friend Allie Brown who is in my school dance troupe. She said I should talk to you if I had the courage to do it."

"Tell Allie not to tell anyone about your conversation."

"I already told her it was a secret, and she's good at being confidential."

The detectives dropped Sue Montgomery off a block from her home, and watched and waited to make sure she made it into the house. This appeared to be the breakthrough they had been waiting for.

"Just think about it, Ewart. Allie Brown knows this secret. Wow, it's amazing how these attacks all have been somehow connected to the Browns. What did they ever do to have these awful things happen to them? I know for a fact that Billy Smith was harassing Allie. It was her father who let the police know Billy was harassing girls at the school. Other than Allie, the girls were all too scared to tell the school officials.

It's almost like God was on the Browns' side when Billy was killed. I heard he had been threatening Jerry Brown, too. Did you know he attacked Allie and Jerry's mom with a baseball bat, giving her a broken arm and wrist?"

Detective Ewart answered, "Well, I don't know if God is on their side. But it must make the Browns feel better to not have to worry about another revenge attack from Billy. I didn't know he had attacked Mrs. Brown. What a cowardly thing to do. She's lucky to be alive. Do we have the DNA samples and hair back from the Smith crime scene yet? They're having the funeral for Billy Smith this Monday at 2 p.m. Sometimes the murderers come to the funeral, so we need to be there, too. I am hoping to get our witness to be able to point them out in a police lineup."

"You're right, one of us needs to be there. I'm starving. Ewart, do you want to go to the steak house and eat? Usually it's easy to get a table there."

"I'm exhausted. I just need to go home and sleep. I will see you tomorrow at eight," Detective Ewart replied.

Detective Kline looked down at the floor and said, "I get it. I guess I'll go home and have some eggs and toast."

Chapter 25

I t was Thursday afternoon. Debra Broadmoor and the Browns were at Cornerstone Church for the weekly prayer meeting. Allie was going to babysit her little sister so Scott's parents could come and pray as well. Since it was spring break, many of their families at the church were on vacation. Today, there were only the four Browns, Debra Broadmoor, and Beth Ames, their 90-year-old prayer warrior, at the prayer gathering.

As the meeting got under way Pastor Jacob Brown led the initial prayers. First, they thanked Jesus for protecting all the Brown family. After this, they had a general thanksgiving prayer for all the good things going on in everyone's lives.

"Now, Scott, how can we pray for you?" his father Jacob asked.

"Dad, I need prayers for me to heal the memory of the terrible fight with Billy Smith. I keep reliving it in my mind. Every night I have nightmares about the fight but I try not to yell out. Sometimes, I go and sleep on the couch so I won't disturb Sandy. It's been a very hard thing to deal with."

"Here, Scott, why don't you sit on this chair in the middle of the group. Will this be all right with you? Vera, dear, would you stand behind Scott and put your hand on his shoulder? Debra, can you put your hand on his other shoulder? Beth and Sandy, you can just pray in your seats."

Jacob prayed, "Dear Jesus, we invite you come into this memory that keeps replaying in Scott's mind. I ask you cleanse the memory and heal him of the trauma. Jesus, we ask you to help him sense your presence there in that memory."

"Scott, do you sense Jesus' presence in the memory with you? What's Jesus doing?"

"Oh, Dad, it's so amazing. I see Sandy on the ground and suddenly

Jesus Christ is lying on top of Sandy, protecting her from the blows. There are two big, white angels stopping Billy Smith from hitting her again. This one huge angel grabs Jerry's arm to make sure that he doesn't kill Billy. The other angel is protecting Billy's head. Jesus told me he made sure that Billy didn't go into a coma because he was still hoping to save him.

"Jesus Christ also said Jerry has important things to do in his life, and he loves him very much. That's why he has protected him in both assaults. He said he is very pleased with Josh who was willing to save his mom, even though the attacker was so much larger than him. Jesus says I don't need to feel guilty for aggressively defending Sandy. He says the more times I forgive Billy Smith, the sooner the nightmares will go away."

Sandy Brown started sobbing loudly. Scott went over to her and gently touched her right arm.

"Dad, we need to pray for my wife, Sandy. She's been through a terrible trauma. I've only been concentrating on what happened to me. She didn't even do anything, and yet she's the victim here," Scott said in a whisper.

"Okay, Scott. Are you sure you don't need any more prayer? How's that bad memory now?"

"Dad, it feels like it was cleaned up. I feel better. So, can we pray for Sandy? Debra, I sense God would like you to lead this prayer. Is that okay, Sandy?"

Sandy looked down at the carpet and wiped her eyes with the tissue that Vera gave her. Then she nodded her head.

Jacob said, "Just a minute, Scott, I keep hearing this scripture from Psalm 126 for Sandy that those who sow with tears will reap with songs of joy. I pray this for our whole family. Okay, Debra, go ahead please."

Vera came and stood behind Sandy and put her hand on her heathy shoulder. Debra was crying with Sandy as she put her arms around her. "Yes, I'll pray. Dear Lord Jesus, Sandy has been attacked even though she didn't do anything wrong. Lord Jesus, we ask for you to touch her left arm and wrist, and heal them quickly. I pray she would sense you and feel your peace that passes all understanding, Lord Jesus. Thank you for saving Sandy's life, and for loving her with an everlasting love. You are so pleased with how she loves and serves her family. I pray this night she will have a restful sleep according to Psalms 3 and 4. Lord, I pray she will be able to forgive Billy Smith for attacking her. Be with her now, and take away the physical and emotional pain. In your name, Jesus. Amen."

Sandy said in a quiet voice, "Dear Jesus, help me to forgive Billy."

Jacob said, "Sometimes it takes a long time to do this from the heart, but Jesus can help you start this process of forgiveness."

Sandy prayed, "Jesus, you know it's so hard for me to forgive Billy. Now he's dead. So, I can't even do this in person. There's no closure. Please, Lord Jesus, I don't feel like forgiving him. Please help me be willing. Thank you so much for saving my life, Jesus. Please help me to give all my pain and bitterness to you. Help me to treat my family better, and be kinder, even when I'm in pain."

She continued to sit in her chair, crying. Scott was kneeling down beside her with his hand on her good shoulder weeping and Debra was doing the same on the other side of her chair, praying under her breath. Vera found the Kleenex box, giving it to Scott and Sandy. The other prayer members continued to pray quietly in their seats.

Vera prayed in closing, "Lord Jesus, thank you for answering our prayers here today. We know Sandy and Scott still have many months of healing ahead of them. We thank you for the emotional and physical healing which started today. Lord, be with them, and give them and the whole family a good night's sleep tonight."

Pastor Jacob said, "Our hour is up and I wonder if Sandy needs to get some rest after having this session?"

Sandy answered, "Normally I could keep going for hours, but with the broken arm and wrist, I do need to go home to rest. Thanks so much to everybody for praying for me and Scott. I feel like I have had emotional surgery. I'm exhausted."

Scott said to his dad, "I really appreciate all you're doing for us and thank you for being willing to preach this Sunday. With 40 years of experience, I guess you can do a guest preaching spot for me." And he smiled.

Then Scott started chuckling, and his dad laughed back. Everyone left the church feeling rested and returned home for dinner.

It was now Sunday morning and the entire Brown family was at Cornerstone Church for the ten a.m. service. Allie had volunteered to help in the Sunday school downstairs with Charity. Josh was at the youth church in the side room, and the rest of the family was in the front pew. Sandy had been nervous to go to church but her mother-in-law had persuaded Sandy that the church loved her, and would want to make sure she was okay. Jerry was sitting at the end of the pew, looking bored. He didn't understand why the place was full. There were people there he had never seen before.

The first song they sang was *"Awesome God,"* which Jerry really liked, so he sang loudly. Next, they sang *"Great and Mighty is He,"* which had a great rhythm and a drum solo. The last song of the set was *"How Great Thou Art,"* so Grandma Vera sang out enthusiastically on that one. After the announcements, it was time for the sermon.

Pastor Jacob Brown told the church all about the tragedy with Billy Smith, and the fact he was now dead. He told everyone how hard it had been for the entire family to come to grips with this tragedy, especially the assault on Sandy. Some may have felt the only good that came from this misfortune was Billy Smith was dead. Pastor Brown said he had a different perspective. He said he hoped that someone had been able to tell Billy before he died that Jesus loved him and wanted him to come to heaven with him. "Jesus loves everyone, even those people who have violently hurt other people. Like Billy Smith, we have all done things wrong. Pastor Scott, my son, was told by the police that Billy was telling everyone he knew that he would get revenge. He was out to get the Brown family, and he did."

Pastor Jacob continued, "Unlike Billy, hopefully you have recognized your weaknesses and your mistakes. You may be thinking that you don't do bad things like Billy Smith. But we hurt others and ourselves through our own selfish desires. Sometimes, as Paul put it in Romans 7, we do things we shouldn't do, like eating too much when we are overweight, gossiping about others, or continuing to smoke when we have trouble breathing. Either way, God wants you to ask Him for forgiveness. We don't know if Billy Smith ever asked God to forgive him, but you can do this today. Don't you want to be sure you'll be in heaven with Jesus Christ? He loves you too much to let you continue in your selfish ways. Come to him today."

"Let's pray. Dear Jesus Christ, I want you to come into my life. I'm sorry for my mistakes. I ask you to forgive me. Help me to forgive those people who have hurt me. People who have said mean things to me or stolen from me. Thank you, Lord Jesus that when I ask you to forgive me, you are pleased to do it. I believe in you and want to go to heaven to be with you when I die. In your name, Jesus. Amen."

When Pastor Jacob was finished speaking, the final song, As the Deer Pants, started. After the service was over, Jerry turned around to see who was still there. He was amazed to see people wiping tears away from their eyes. Jerry was thrilled to see his friend Jim who came running up to Jerry, and punched him on the shoulder.

"Hey, Jerry. Your grandpa sure tells a cool story. I didn't know that about Billy. He was one scary dude. I'm amazed none of you were killed by that crazy bat-wielding fiend. You know I prayed that prayer with your grandpa, and I feel better inside. I was wrong to tease you about Samantha. You probably know I was lying about all the guys in the music class. She actually only went out with Shaun but she dumped him two weeks later. I'm glad she's treating you right."

"Wow, Jim. Thanks. It's great you prayed today with my grandpa. Maybe you can come to youth group with me on Wednesday. We have a supper club that ends at 7:30, so you can still get home to do your homework. I'm amazed you had the guts to apologize to me. Awesome, man. Let's go get some food at Denny's."

"Okay, dude. Let's do it." And they walked out side by side.

Scott and Sandy were elated with Grandpa Jacob's sermon. They were both amazed to see neighbors and friends who had never come to church before at the service. Scott wondered if they were publicity seekers or if they were there in solidarity with his family. Many of them appeared to have tears in their eyes. He wondered if some of his friends from the Eagle's Nest Church had come to support them. They loved to pray for healing for people.

Scott had been pleased to see Jerry's friend Jim there. He noticed they left immediately after the service. Sandy said they were going to

Denny's to hang out before school started again tomorrow. Allie had really enjoyed helping the small children with their crafts in the Sunday school. Charity was very happy and proud to have had her pretty, big sister there in her class to help her make her clay elephant for Noah's ark. The children were thrilled the teenagers had made them a papier-mâché ark. Josh had enjoyed making it, and was thinking they could make one for Charity's birthday party in September.

Chapter 26

The Brown children were going back to school on Tuesday. After the dramatic events during spring break, the Browns were given an extra day off on Monday by their school counselors. Instead, all three were to go to individual counseling with Kerry Andrews. Charity, as the youngest with no specific trauma, would start back to school on Monday.

It was also the day of Billy Smith's funeral. Scott wondered if there would be anyone there, besides Rue Smith and himself. He was amazed the Roman Catholic Bishop had agreed to say a funeral Mass for Billy. Sandy wanted to go to the funeral, but the rest of the family nixed that idea. Only Grandpa Jacob and Scott would make it to the service.

The whole family, including Josh, had now gone to see the counselor. Josh didn't seem to be affected by the events, or else he was very frozen. Unlike the rest of the family, he didn't complain of nightmares. Charity, thank God, didn't have the nightmares as she hadn't been involved in any of the goings-on. Since the prayer the other week, Scott seemed to either have fewer nightmares, or he couldn't remember them if he did. Sandy wasn't calling out in her sleep anymore, either. She looked much more relaxed now. Her eyes were no longer filled with fear and pain. In a few weeks, she was going to try and work a few hours at the medical clinic. She said she could type with one hand. It would just be slow. She also said she could answer the office phone using the loudspeaker. Scott was not sure how well that would work out, given the confidentiality of the medical clinic. But he figured the staff would let her know.

It was now 1 p.m. on Monday afternoon, so Scott and his father Jacob prepared to leave in order to make it downtown to the Roman Catholic Cathedral on time. After they found parking six blocks away, they hurried into the church. The usher asked them which particular funeral Mass they were attending. When they replied "the Billy Smith funeral Mass," they were taken to a small side chapel.

Looking around, Scott noticed Detective Cassidy and Detective Kline. Only a few other people were in the chapel. He wondered if they were publicity seekers, as most people who knew him didn't seem to have liked Billy Smith. Just before two, the bishop arrived in his white robes with his chaplain swinging a censer full of incense which sweetened the air. Right at 2 p.m., Janette Bingley, the district reserve officer from the police department, walked down the aisle with Rue Smith, holding her firmly by the arm. Scott noticed she was not wearing any handcuffs. As the funeral was starting, a guy with sunglasses and blond hair sticking out the back of his cap walked in and sat at the back. Beside him were two huge, muscular guys with long, blond hair.

Rue looked beautiful, even though she was a known liar and thief. She was wearing a stylish black hat, black dress, black hose, black handbag, and black shoes. When the Bishop asked her to say some words about the deceased, she immediately stood up. Rue appeared to cry, holding a large black handkerchief up to her eyes. Rue explained Billy was only her half brother, so he hadn't been given much attention from Rue's mother when they were little. She went on to say both her dad and her grandfather had beaten him for no reason. All the beatings must have affected Billy's brain. Then Rue sat down abruptly. When the detectives looked at her, they observed there were no tears in her eyes. In fact, she seemed strangely happy.

The funeral Mass was over quickly. Most of the people there were not Roman Catholic and not eligible to receive communion. When the service was over, Janette Bingley and Rue Smith walked off to another part of the cathedral. Scott and his father assumed they were going to use the restroom.

Rue was very pleased with the short but beautiful funeral Mass. Billy didn't really deserve it, but if it helped her make an escape from prison, it would be worth it. Now if she could only trick this police woman into giving her some freedom.

When they got to the restroom, they found there was only room inside for one person at a time. It was a very old church, so restrooms had not been a priority when it was built. Rue was thrilled with this discovery. She went through the door and locked it. Looking around, she saw a small, open window. When she had flushed the toilet, she quietly grabbed the window and pulled it open as far as it would go. She had carefully hidden a change of clothes in her large black handbag. Quickly changing into another outfit, she put the black handkerchief over her hair, and squeezed through the window.

The police woman asked her through the door if she was okay. Rue replied she would be out in a few minutes. Once outside she quickly looked around, noticing she was in a back alley. She had on her white hat, white shirt, white pants, and black sunglasses. She was glad she had her running shoes on. The black clothes she had been wearing she'd left in the restroom trash can, hidden underneath other garbage. She started running down the alley.

Janette Bingley yelled, "Rue, how're you doing? Are you okay? Open this door immediately, or I'll have to get the policemen to break it down."

There was no response to her command. Janette ran back to the funeral chapel, searching for the police detectives. Detective Cassidy was still there talking to Scott. She told him that he needed to come with her quickly as she was afraid that Rue Smith had escaped. Detective Cassidy ran ahead and yelled, banging at the restroom door. The janitor heard them shouting, and came to unlock the door. There was nobody in the bathroom. She was gone.

Detective Cassidy phoned the police station to put out another APB on Rue Smith. He felt embarrassed and responsible since he had agreed that she could wear her street clothes to the funeral. The other detectives said it wasn't his fault. They assured him it was common decency to let prisoners wear their street clothes to a family funeral. Everyone at the police station, however, admired her ingenuity at being able to escape from a tiny 12-by-12-inch square window. They were still shaking their heads over that one. Janette Bingley also felt ashamed, but as Detective Cassidy had reminded her, Rue Smith had tricked many men and women over the last few years. This was nothing new.

Detective Kline, meanwhile, was carefully observing the three odd-looking men who were sitting in the back pew at the funeral. Since she was a woman, they were not threatened as she followed them out the door. When the detective left the church, she nodded knowingly at a dirty vagrant before getting into her unmarked police car. Back at the office, she spoke with her partner, Detective Ewart, telling him all about the funeral.

She mentioned how strange it had been to be at a funeral where there were so few people. No one except Rue Smith seemed to care about her brother. It was sad to have such a small crowd there.

Detective Ewart had just told Detective Kline they had received the results back on the DNA hair samples at Billy Smith's crime scene. Thomas Green and Paul Blake were both in the police database. It was their hair and skin which was discovered at the murder scene. Also, some bits of cotton fiber had been found. So, they were hoping to uncover where the gang hangout was located. If they could find some blue jeans at that place which matched the cotton fibers, it should be enough to indict them. Perhaps they had not intended to kill Billy, but that's what had occurred.

Detective Kline couldn't believe the nerve of those three to actually turn up at the funeral. Maybe they wanted to confirm Billy Smith was actually dead. It could be they thought he had just been hurt, and was still roaming around somewhere. It was exciting to see that she and Detective Ewart were correct. They were impatient for the police chief to give them permission to raid the hangout. They were so near to catching the culprits that they could almost taste it.

Chapter 27

I t wasn't as simple as Rue had thought to have a clean getaway. She had had to walk for miles before she was able to find the dumpster behind her former apartment. Rue didn't know who lived in her apartment now, but that didn't matter. The money and gun she had hidden were still there behind the trash bin, buried behind a brick at the bottom of the wall. She just had to hide and wait behind it until it was dark. Her plan was to use her nail clippers as a knife and dig out her stash.

Finally, the sun went down, and she got to work. For a moment, she had to stop digging at the wall, as she heard a police siren go by. If she could just get her money and her gun, she would take a bus to Boise, Idaho and get her passport out of the bank. All she needed was a lucky break, and she would be completely free again. Just as she was pulling the bag full of money out of the hole, she heard "Police! Come out with your hands in the air."

Rue was so livid she could spit. Where was her gun? Ah, now she could feel it in her hands. There was no way she was going back to jail. In desperation, she decided to shoot her way out.

How could it be they had found her already?

It was dark out now, and the officers couldn't get a clear view of her. Detective Cassidy wanted her to stand trial for grand larceny. He warned the police to not shoot her unless they had to.

"Rue Smith, come out now or we will shoot you!" Detective Cassidy yelled.

"I'm coming, Detective, don't aim at me. Here I am."

As she stood up, they saw her in her white hat and clothes running around the dumpster in the dark, shooting wildly at the police. They returned her fire. There was chaos, with bullets pinging all over the brick wall and dumpster. It was like a laser light show. Two minutes later, they found Rue Smith lying on the ground behind the dumpster, bleeding. Detective Cassidy also lay on the ground on the other side of it, with a bullet hole in his shoulder. Rue Smith had shot him. Janette Bingley called for ambulances. She got down on her knees and covered Rue's abdomen with her hand, trying to stop the massive bleeding.

Janette Bingley said gently, "Come on, Rue. Don't die on me now. We just found you again. Hang on."

She bent her head down to hear what Rue was saying.

"I'm not going back to prison. Let me die, please. I have no hope if I am stuck in a prison cell. Thanks for being kind to me, Janette."

As ambulances came racing around the corner with the sirens shrieking, it appeared Rue had died. The paramedics ran over and checked the bleeding. They said she was close to bleeding to death, but they could try to revive her at the hospital. They quickly gave her oxygen and wrapped her up. There was a chance they could save her. They rushed her off to the nearest emergency ward hooked up to an intravenous drip. Other paramedics bandaged Detective Cassidy's injured shoulder, taking him away in the other ambulance. Before he left, the detective made sure there was a police presence at the emergency ward with Rue Smith. Janette Bingley went in the other ambulance with Detective Cassidy to a trauma ward in another hospital further away.

Janette said to Detective Cassidy, "Rue Smith told me she didn't want to live if she had to be in a prison cell. I think she was surprised we were able to catch her. She didn't realize how much noise she was making digging the money and gun out from the brick wall. It's a good thing the new owners phoned 911, complaining of all the noise going on outside their apartment this late at night."

Holding Detective Cassidy's hand in the ambulance, Janette said, "Detective, I'm so sorry I let her get away. Who knew she was so skinny that she could get through such a tiny window? When we checked out the church premises, we were sure there was no way she would be able to get through that window. I hope you have no permanent damage to your shoulder. I regret this happened to you."

"Well, Janette, I did have a bullet hole in that shoulder before. Oh, it hurts."

Detective Cassidy groaned in pain, before passing out. Janette was glad the paramedics were in the ambulance monitoring him. They told her he should be all right, as he hadn't lost much blood. Arriving at the trauma ward, he was taken right in. Twenty minutes later, Detective Cassidy was in the OR having his surgery.

An hour later, homicide detectives Kline and Ewart arrived in the waiting room of Detective Cassidy's hospital. Detective Kline had been monitoring Brutus and his thugs. One of the undercover police officers, disguised as a vagrant, was now following them to discover where they hung out. The detectives told Janette that they were sure they would soon be able to arrest Brutus and his two associates for murder. She was thankful there was something positive for a change.

Meanwhile, Rue Smith was in surgery. The hospital staff had determined that her blood type was O positive, and had immediately started restoring her blood supply with a blood transfusion. The surgeon hoped he might be able to save her life, as the two bullets had missed her vital arteries. Since she had previously had a hysterectomy, she would survive as long as they took out her spleen. Eight hours later, the surgery was finished. Rue had many lines coming out of her arms, including the intravenous for pain, the drip for dehydration and another blood transfusion being pumped into her. It would be several hours before the nurses in ICU knew whether she would survive.

Because Providence Sacred Heart hospital was a Roman Catholic institution, the chaplain had been notified to give her the last rites if they determined she was dying. The chaplain went to her room and prayed for her. When the Bishop heard that Rue Smith had been shot, he had informed Pastor Brown. Pastor Brown asked if he could go and visit her. The bishop didn't know whether the police would allow that. Pastor Brown phoned Detective Cassidy, but the voicemail came on instead. He wondered if Detective Cassidy was at the hospital waiting to find out the fate of Rue Smith.

It was eight the next morning. Scott was up and about, getting ready to go to Sacred Heart Hospital to attempt to visit Rue Smith. Someone needed to let her know Jesus Christ loved her. Twenty minutes later, he arrived at the hospital, and asked for Rue's room. The receptionist said as an ICU patient, only the police or family were allowed to go to see her as she was in custody.

"Are you a relative, sir? Only relatives are allowed to visit."

"No, but I know Rue through her brother. I attended her brother's funeral yesterday. Also, I'm a pastor, and would like to go and pray with her."

"All right. You can go up to ICU and see if the police will let you in to see her. I'm sure she could use your prayers. It's on the fifth floor on the west side."

Scott took the elevator up to 5W, and walked through to the ICU ward. The nurse at the station asked whom he wanted to see. He replied he had come to pray for Rue Smith. The nurse said he was welcome to pray, but he couldn't go in her room. He could look through the window at her.

Scott asked, "Where are the police officers? Can I speak to them, please?"

The nurse looked on her chart, and went down the hall to check. She came back with Detective Ewart from homicide who was very surprised to see Pastor Brown.

Detective Ewart said, "How can I help you, Pastor?"

"Hello, Detective. I'm Pastor Scott Brown. I don't know Rue personally, but I know of her. I was at the funeral for her brother yesterday. I was hoping you would allow me to pray for Rue. I have had success praying for the critically wounded in the past. What do you think?"

"It's true we would like her to survive. She's not waking up, and we don't know whether she ever will. I guess if I go with you, it would be all right for you to pray in her room. Just don't touch her or any of the equipment."

Scott was pleased the police detective was willing to take a chance on him. He didn't know Detective Ewart was a Christian who also believed in the power of prayer. Within two minutes, they arrived at her room. Scott could barely see Rue due to the many tubes and bandages covering her body. Quietly, Scott started praying for her under his breath. He felt the peace of Jesus Christ enter the room. Rue opened her eyes and stared right at Scott. She started whispering something, so the police detective allowed Scott to go over closer to Rue's bedside.

"I saw you at the funeral yesterday. Thanks for coming. Are you going to pray for me? I think I'm dying, but I'm afraid to die. I don't want to go to hell. My grandma told me all about it when I was a little girl. Please pray."

"Rue, I'm Pastor Brown. I know you don't like my family, but I want to tell you that I forgive you and your brother for all the pain and suffering you have caused my family. It's tough your brother died… Do you know Jesus Christ loves you and wants you to be with him in heaven? All you need to do is say you're sorry and ask him to forgive you."

Rue whispered in a small voice, "Pastor, I'm no good. No one could ever love me now. It's too late for me. How could God love me after all the terrible things I've done? Could you just pray that if I have to die, it won't hurt so much? I'm in lots of pain, and feeling scared."

"Lord Jesus, I pray you'll take away the great pain Rue is feeling right now. Do you know that God the Father, Jesus Christ the Son, and the Holy Spirit all love you? But in order for you to get into heaven, you need to repent. You need to tell Jesus you're sorry for all the people you tricked and all the money and confidential files you stole."

Rue replied again, "I'm too tired, so please leave. Maybe later, I can pray to Jesus. Right now, I'm in too much pain. Can you get the nurse to come and give me more pain medication?"

"Okay. I'll tell the nurse."

Detective Ewart escorted Pastor Brown out of the ICU room and down the hall. One of the nurses went to Rue Smith's room, giving her extra pain medication by mouth. The nurses were amazed she had awakened for those few minutes and actually spoke to the pastor.

As they were walking down the hall, the homicide detective smiled at the pastor and shook his hand.

"Maybe if you come back tomorrow, if Rue's still alive, she might be willing to tell you her secrets. I'm surprised she was willing to talk to you as she has told Detective Cassidy how much she hates you. By the way, you need to also remember to pray for him. He is in ICU at

Lawson Hospital. Rue Smith shot him in the shoulder. We're hoping he will make a complete recovery."

"I'm upset to hear this. Our whole family will pray for him. Do you think he would allow me to come and see him in the hospital? I'll check tomorrow and find out if I can go in and see him there."

The following morning at ten, Scott and his father went over to Lawson Hospital to see if they would be permitted to visit Detective Cassidy. The nurse on the ICU floor said no, this was not possible. Scott asked to speak to the police guard at Detective Cassidy's hospital room. The guard came over and spoke to Scott. He agreed to Scott's request that Detective Cassidy be asked whether he would agree to see the two pastors. Two minutes later the guard came out of the room and waved, beckoning for them to come into Detective Cassidy's room.

Poor Detective Cassidy was hooked up to several machines, but at least he was awake. He looked very groggy and pale. The two pastors entered the room, and instantly started praying silently.

Scott said, "How are you? I'm so sorry this happened to you. Would it be all right with you if we prayed for your shoulder, Detective? This is my father, Pastor Jacob Brown."

"Yes, of course. I need all the help I can get. This shoulder was injured before, so I'm worried I will not be able to go back on active duty. It hurts like the dickens. The trouble is the painkillers make it so I have trouble sleeping. Last night I dreamt that Rue Smith had come into this room and tried to kill me with a tire iron. The nurse had to wake me up to stop the screaming and let me know it wasn't real."

"Oh, that sounds like a terrible nightmare. My father is very good at praying for healing. He prayed for me when I was so burdened by Billy Smith. Now I feel much lighter, and the nightmares are gone. Will you let my dad pray for you?"

Detective Cassidy turned his head and said to Pastor Jacob, "Hello, sir. I would be glad to have prayers for the healing of my shoulder. It's really in pain. Apparently, they had to dig out a bullet which had almost gone all the way through my shoulder. I'm afraid I will have limited use of my shoulder after I get out of the hospital. Pastor Jacob, if you want to pray for me, please go ahead. I don't go to church myself, sir, but I do respect your son."

Pastor Jacob prayed, "Dear Jesus, we come here this morning to ask for healing for Detective Cassidy. Lord, you love him very much and are pleased at the way he protects the public here in Spokane. Please speed up the healing of his shoulder. May the ligaments and sinew heal quickly, and may there not be any scarring on top of old scars. I pray he will know how much you love him, Lord Jesus. We pray he can have good sleep and no more nightmares. Amen."

Scott could see the detective was becoming drowsy and peaceful. He was pleased he had thought to bring his father with him. His dad was a great prayer warrior. Scott prayed as well under his breath that the detective would know Jesus Christ who could set him free from his cynical nature.

Chapter 28

Everyone in Jerry's class was trying to stay awake after being on spring break for a week. Math was always a difficult subject, especially now when they were into a new chapter. He was glad Lewis would be over later that night and explain the new concepts to him. It was hard not to daydream in math about seeing Samantha again. He had been so happy to go to the movies with her. If only she would get along better with Allie. They always seemed to butt heads. Samantha would disagree with whatever Allie said and vice versa.

After lunch, came music class. They were starting a new unit on classical music. Jerry was concerned he'd fall asleep in class. Mr. Rush stepped into the classroom with Samantha rushing in right behind him. Luckily, Jerry had saved a seat for her.

Mr. Rush said, "Why were you late, Samantha? You're supposed to be here before me, not after me."

Samantha turned red and looked down at her sneakers. Jerry gave her a nudge.

She looked up. "Excuse me, Mr. Rush. I now have math just before this class, and it's a long way between classes."

"Okay, Samantha. Try not to do it again. You don't want to have detention, do you?"

"No, sir. I'll try to be on time."

"Jerry, what do you know about the classical musician, Mozart?

"Well, sir, he was a child prodigy. He could already play and write music by the age of four. His father had him travel all over Europe playing his songs on his little pianoforte."

"That's right, Jerry. I didn't know you had a classical background."

"I don't, sir, but my father is a classical pianist."

"Okay, everyone be ready to listen, and tell me if you can name this symphonic work."

Jerry was relieved he wasn't asked any more questions, as the sum of his knowledge for classical music history was Mozart. He hoped they weren't just going to listen or have to read music scores for the rest of the year.

After school, he waited for Samantha while she auditioned for the *Beauty and the Beast* musical. She was trying out for the part of Belle. Jerry remembered Allie wanted that part too. Samantha told him that she should know in a couple of weeks. Jerry waved at her as she came out of the auditorium and walked her home.

As Jerry sauntered into his house, there was Allie sitting at the kitchen table eating an apple. She appeared relaxed and happy. It was such a relief that Billy Smith was dead. He'd never be able to hurt her again. She looked up at her brother and grinned.

"Jerry, I just auditioned for the part of Belle in *Beauty and the Beast*. I'm pretty sure I will get it since I'm the best singer and dancer at the school." She smiled, giving him a wink.

He smiled back, then looked seriously at her, "Allie, they don't always pick people the way you hope. You don't really think you're the best singer in the school, do you?"

"Of course, I don't. But Jerry, don't rain on my parade. I've been praying that I'll get the part. Chill, dude. God likes to answer my prayers. I'm also praying Lewis will get the part of the Beast. I think we would look great together."

"But Allie, God doesn't always answer prayers that way. There are school politics involved as well. They don't usually let the same person be the lead in every play or musical. How many musicals has Lewis been in? Doesn't experience count for something? Maybe I should audition for a part myself."

"You, Jerry? What part could you play? Gaston?"

"Maybe. I've seen it enough times. Samantha was encouraging me to try out. Why not? They want him to be good-looking, and I've been told by many girls how handsome I am."

"Oh, you mean Samantha. I think she's prejudiced in your favor," replied Allie while she poked him on the shoulder. "But you are quite good-looking, so go ahead and audition. Do you think you'll have time? How's math going for you now? You need to keep your marks up, you know."

"Yes, ma'am." Jerry saluted Allie and gave her a grin. "School has just started again, so why don't we wait and see how I do this term. Besides, we don't know if I will get the part."

Two weeks later, auditions closed. The notice on the bulletin outside the drama room had the following posting:

Belle: Sue Montgomery	*Mrs. Potts:* Allie Brown
The Beast: Luke Asher	*Lumiere:* Lewis Lee
Gaston: Jerry Brown	*First Milkmaid:* Samantha Jones
Le Fou: Jim Lawlor	

Jerry looked forward to singing with Jim. The roles of the plates, cups, and other chorus members would be acted by eighth and ninth grade students. The dance teacher was going to help with the rehearsals. Samantha said everyone in the dance class was looking forward to being in the play. The rehearsals would take place after school, starting on April 15. Here was the best news. The music class would all be involved in the production. Then starting in May, they would have rehearsals during music class. The production would run for three nights: Wednesday, June 1st, Thursday, June 2nd, and Friday, June 3rd.

Jerry was very excited to have a role in the play, and be spending more time with Samantha. He was surprised that Sue was cast as Belle, but it made sense to have Luke be the Beast since he was so tall. Also, unlike Lewis, who was also very tall, he knew how to dance. In basketball, you needed to have some dance moves to make it to the basket before the other team stole the ball. He had listened to Luke's singing audition, and it was amazing. Allie was shocked she didn't get to be Belle, but was pleased she still had a solo in the musical. His mom told Jerry that Allie had come home and cried. But she was getting used to the idea of only being Mrs. Potts. She was attempting to forgive Sue for winning the starring role.

Sue's dad was home from Alaska, so she had time to be in the play. He'd had a good fishing season so now Sue didn't have to work after school and on weekends. Everyone at school was involved in the musical in some way. There were 50 people acting in the play. But those students who were not acting in *Beauty and the Beast* were making scenery and doing local advertising. Even the senior class math department was having a car rally to make money for the production. The dance instructor told Allie that she needed her help with the choreography. Jerry thought this must make her feel better since she didn't get the lead. Allie had confessed that she didn't realize Sue was a good singer. Her friend had a wonderful range as she could hit all the high and the low notes and could easily be heard from the back of the auditorium.

It was now the first weekend of April. Jerry had just walked in the kitchen door on Friday afternoon. He was glad his mom was staying home for a change. It was too bad she had a broken arm, but she seemed less stressed, not having to juggle so many balls in the air.

Allie was not home from school yet but he'd seen her walking slowly along, holding hands with Lewis. He was about to tell his mom that he and Jim were heading off to the mall. It was Friday night, and he hoped to meet Samantha and her girlfriends there, as well.

"Mom, hey Mom, I'm home. Where are you?" Jerry called.

He walked through the house, calling for her.

He hurried up the stairs and knocked on her bedroom door. No answer, the bathroom, no answer. Running down to the basement, he looked through all those rooms, too. She wasn't there either. Jerry thought: Of course, she must be in the living room. Why isn't she answering me? She must be having a nap since no one else is home. Charity had gone with Dad and his grandparents to Seattle this afternoon to watch Josh run his race tomorrow. Jerry was starting to sweat and feel anxious.

As Jerry walked into the living room, he found his mom lying on the carpet. It looked like she had fallen off the couch. Her face was flushed, and when he touched her forehead, it was very hot. She didn't respond when he called her name. Where was Allie? She was good at this kind of emergency. He wasn't even old enough to drive. He looked at the cast on his mom's arm and saw the flesh around the top of the cast was black and blue, looking very swollen. He decided it would be wise to immediately call an ambulance and get her back to the hospital.

Hearing Allie and Lewis come into the kitchen, Jerry said, "Allie, come quickly into the living room. Mom needs help. I think she needs to go to the hospital."

"Chill, I'm coming right now, stop yelling," Allie said as she came around the corner into the living room. When she saw her mom unconscious on the floor, she started hyperventilating and Lewis had to calm her down. He took control of the situation, telling her to take deep breaths and blow them out slowly.

"Jerry, phone 911 at once. It looks like your mom has an infection in her arm. She needs to go to Lawson Hospital. Call your Dad in Seattle and leave a message for him on your grandparents' answering machine. Allie, chill out, Babe. Remember, deep breaths. Can you get a damp cloth for your mom and some ice packs from the kitchen to cool her down while we wait for the ambulance?"

Allie nodded and ran to the bathroom for a cold cloth and then the kitchen for ice packs. Lewis put the cloth on her mother's forehead and the ice packs on the top of her head. They were hoping the ambulance would arrive quickly.

Allie pulled herself together, and went searching for her mom's purse while Jerry dialed 911. They said they would be there in ten minutes. Jerry was glad Charity and Josh were in Seattle, so he didn't have to worry about looking after them, too. He was surprised Allie had lost it like that. She was usually so reliable and good in emergencies. Thank God, Lewis was there to think calmly.

Lewis said, "I hope your dad left the car keys for you, Allie, so you can drive. Or if you want, I can drive us in your car to the hospital, as soon as the ambulance comes for your mom. Does she have a set of keys in her purse?"

Allie found her mom's purse, and the car keys and ID were in it. Sandy continued to be unresponsive. This made Allie cry while Jerry nervously tapped his toe. Lewis stood there quietly and gave her a tissue while they waited for the ambulance. He put his arm around Allie, patting her on the shoulder. The paramedics arrived and started asking questions. None of the teens knew how long Sandy had been unconscious or how she had fallen down. When the paramedics checked her temperature, they started moving very quickly as she had a temperature of 104 F. They began an IV drip in her healthy arm, and strapped her onto the stretcher. They said they were rushing her to the Trauma Center at Lawson Hospital.

Allie brought her mother's purse as Jerry locked the doors with their mom's keys, and everyone jumped into the family station wagon. Lewis drove and they followed the ambulance to the hospital. The ambulance was already there by the time the teens made it to the Trauma Center at the hospital. The attendant taking Sandy Brown's statistics instructed Allie to sit down and fill out the patient admittance form. The attendant discovered they already had Sandy's information from the previous admittance a few weeks ago.

Thirty minutes later, one of the senior interns came out to the reception area to let Sandy's family know what was going on with their mother. The admitting doctor said they needed to remove her cast to determine what was happening to her arm. He said they suspected she had an infection in her arm from her wrist up to her elbow. They had taken some lab samples to find out what the infection was. He also asked them when Mr. Brown would get to the hospital.

"Doctor, our father is on his way to Seattle for a track meet for our brother, Josh. He won't be home till tomorrow night. I'll try phoning him again at the phone booth here in the hospital. We don't know if he has made it to Seattle yet," Jerry replied.

"Good thing you brought your mom in here when you did. She's very ill. I'm surprised you didn't notice this earlier in the week."

"We've been busy back at school and she's not up when we leave in the morning. Mom always had a blanket covering the arm above the cast, so we didn't see the discoloring. I'm not sure it was on her arm until today. She seemed to be better earlier in the week. Allie, what do you think?"

"I agree with Josh. If she was sick earlier, she was doing a good job of hiding it. My mom does like to be a martyr sometimes, so maybe she was just hiding the pain and taking her pain medication for relief."

The doctor replied, "Phone your father and see what he knows about the situation. Maybe she fell just today, and something got caught on her cast, bumping her skin which made it infected."

Jerry agreed, "Okay, doctor, I'll phone Dad and find out what he knows."

The doctor left, and all three teens went to find places to sit in the waiting room. Allie and her boyfriend found two seats together and sat, holding hands and looking worried. Jerry preferred to stand, but after 30 minutes, he remembered he needed to find a pay phone. Thankfully Allie had brought his mom's wallet which had enough coins in it to use in the pay phone. It was now five in the evening so Jerry tried phoning Seattle again. This time his grandfather answered the phone.

"Hello, Grandpa? This is Jerry. Is Dad there, please? I need to talk to him, right away."

"Yes, he's right here. Just a moment."

"Hello, Jerry. Is everything all right?"

"Actually, no, it's not, Dad. We had to take Mom to the hospital again as her broken arm was all swollen and bruised. She couldn't even talk to us, and she has a high fever. Did you notice her arm was bruised above the cast?"

"No, I didn't notice any problem with her arm. Do I need to come home immediately? I feel terrible about this."

"Well, Dad, it's strange none of us noticed her bruises and swollen arm. Since you are far away and it will take you hours to get home, why don't you just come home tomorrow as planned? She's safe in the hospital; the doctors are on it. When is Josh's race tomorrow?"

"Let me just look on the program. Josh's race is at eight in the morning and it takes four hours. I wonder if Charity and I could get a plane ride home on an earlier flight. I will phone the airlines right away and see if I can change my flight for Saturday at 3 p.m. Please let me know how things are going or ask the hospital to phone me tonight at this number here in Seattle."

Chapter 29

S cott was stunned to hear Sandy was sick again. He felt like his world was collapsing. She had been fine when they left early that morning. How could she get sick so quickly like that? He didn't want to tell his younger children before the race, but he had to tell his parents so the three of them could be praying for her. It had been over three weeks ago since she had been attacked by Billy Smith and she had appeared to be making a good recovery. Her attitude about life was certainly better.

As he came into his parent's living room, Scott said quietly, "Dad and Mom, I don't want my younger children to know this, yet. Sandy has been taken back to the hospital. There was an infection underneath the cast. Either Jerry or the hospital will phone me in a few hours with an update on her condition."

He looked down at the floor and started to cry. Immediately both his parents got up and put their arms around his shoulders.

His mother said, "Dear Jesus, please heal Sandy. Save her arm and keep her safe. Lord, she has already gone through so much. Please be with not only her, but Allie, and Jerry, too. May they all stay safe. Oh Lord, this is such terrible news. Cover Sandy with your blood protection."

Then his father prayed, "Lord Jesus, we don't know why this has happened, but we know you have the gift of life for us. We pray your life into Sandy. I also pray she doesn't give up. We know you love her. Please cover her and heal her. Surround her with your holy angels. I pray Sandy senses Jesus Christ there with her tonight in that hospital room."

Scott Brown stood there silently and wiped the tears streaming down his face with his sleeve. What a comfort to have his parents' arms around him. It was terribly distressing to not be able to be there with Sandy.

Jerry was right that it would be very upsetting for Josh if his dad missed watching his race. Sandy needed to be in the hospital so she could be properly cared for. Besides, she was unconscious and wouldn't know he wasn't there with her. He would check with the airlines right now and see if he could change the flight time for tomorrow to afternoon instead of the evening.

How could it be that Rue Smith, who had never helped anyone in her life, might be getting better, but his own dear wife, who had never hurt anyone, was sick again? God only knew how this was just because it didn't seem fair at all. He was so grateful to be with his parents who could pray for him when he didn't feel like praying at all. Scott felt like a hypocrite because he didn't feel like praying for Rue Smith, period. Not after her brother was the one who had hurt his dear wife. He was discouraged as he thought he had forgiven Billy and Rue Smith, but it sure didn't feel like that right at this moment. How could he be a pastor if he wasn't willing to pardon those who were unlovable? How could he tell Vicki and Jake Broadmoor to forgive each other when he was having trouble forgiving people himself? Why did God expect him to forgive these people when they really didn't deserve to be forgiven?

Scott sat in the guest bedroom on the one comfortable, old, upholstered armchair. He told God how angry he felt. Despite his efforts to pray, all he could get out was "Help, Lord."

Jesus replied, "Scott, do you know the price I paid for dying for your sins? I couldn't save you or anyone else unless I died on the cross. I died from yours and everyone else's mistakes and selfish desires. Forgiveness is not easy but it's the way of the cross. I love you, son. Come to me, and I will help you forgive your enemies. Don't fret about Sandy. She'll make it."

Scott prayed, "Dear Lord Jesus, I repent of my bad attitude. Help me to forgive everyone, including myself, for my selfishness and mistakes. Help me to be a man of peace. Lord, I pray Charity and I can get on stand-by for the 3 p.m. flight back to Spokane. I pray healing for Sandy. May Josh do well in his race tomorrow. Help Sandy forgive me for not being there with her. Amen."

Scott got into his pajamas and went to lie down on the bed in his parent's guestroom. He was glad Josh and Charity were here with him

173

and his parents were looking after them. Scott sighed and prayed that all the family would have a good night's sleep and keep safe. He didn't know if he would be able to sleep at all.

Jerry, Allie and her friend Lewis had waited till ten p.m., and still had not heard the results of their mother's blood tests. They decided to go home and come back on Saturday morning. Allie dropped Lewis off on the way back home. The hospital said someone would phone their father that night, as soon as they had the results. Their mother was still unconscious, but the nurses explained the doctor had said this was a good thing so she wouldn't knock her sore arm around and injure it further.

Sandy's body looked like it was covered in tubes again. She had the strangest thought she was floating as she could see her body below her. Sandy wondered why she would be in the hospital again. How could she be floating up in the air? Her left arm looked terrible from what she could see. Suddenly, there was a blinding white light in front of her, filling the hospital room.

"Sandy, I have heard your family's prayers and so I'm letting you know it's not your time yet. You must go back. I'm sorry, but you will have lots more pain. It will give you a way to understand people's hurts. You will know how to pray for others' healing of physical and emotional pain. I will give you the gift of healing. I love you, Sandy. Time for you to go back."

Opening her eyes, Sandy tried to turn her head, looking at her left arm. It seemed she remembered talking to the Lord Jesus, but she wasn't sure about that. She wasn't able to see her arm as there were tubes down her throat and she had an oxygen mask on her face—she couldn't even move. She thought to herself, Wow, what did I do to myself this time? And she went back to sleep.

The morning nurse came in. She noted on the monitor that there had been some movement. She didn't notice any other changes, except

Sandy's fever was down and her face was turned to the side. There were still no results back from the biopsy on her arm. It was very black and swollen around the elbow but her hand appeared normal.

It took the lab longer than they expected to get the results back so they didn't phone the Brown residence till nine the next morning.

Allie was up early waiting for the call from the hospital. When the doctor phoned at 9 a.m., he told her that her mother was very sick. The infection in her arm was called necrotizing fasciitis, also known as flesh-eating disease. It had already started destroying part of her mother's forearm. He said to not come and visit until her mother was out of her surgery. They intended to operate right away and try to save what they could of her arm. Allie asked him how her mother could have gotten this infection as she had just been sitting in the house for two weeks. The doctor responded that her mother must have cut her arm on the cast when she fell two days ago. The bacteria on her skin through the cut had spread into her blood system. He said this particular infection spreads through the blood very quickly.

When Allie hung up the phone, she immediately dialed her grandparents' house in Seattle. The phone rang five times until finally her grandmother answered. Allie asked to speak to her dad but was told he was at Josh's track meet. Allie told her grandmother what the doctor from Lawson Hospital had said about her mother. Vera was shocked to hear the terrible news. She said they had already decided she would fly back today with Charity and Allie's dad on the 3 p.m. flight to Spokane. Grandma Vera promised Allie that she would soon be there to help them. Since it was a medical emergency, the airline had made sure they had seats on the plane. Her grandmother told Allie to keep praying and to ask the prayer chain at church to pray for her mother, too. Vera said the three of them would go directly to the hospital as soon as they flew back to Spokane.

Scott was pleased that Josh had finished in second place in his long distance ten-kilometer race. Unfortunately, it was difficult for Scott to celebrate Josh's accomplishment, with his wife Sandy so sick in hospital once again. When his mother had told Scott about Sandy having the flesh-eating disease, he wanted to yell at God. Why was Sandy going through this terrible ordeal? How could God treat her like this? He didn't want Sandy to die, she was too young, and he still needed her. Scott started praying in the spirit for God to save Sandy's life.

Their flight left on time and they were back in Spokane at 4 p.m. Scott had phoned ahead to his daughter Allie, and she had agreed to pick them up from the airport. He had called Lawson Hospital before they left Seattle, but there was no news yet on his wife's surgery outcome. The nurse on duty said the medical team was still in surgery with his wife. His mother was trying to keep Charity interested in her coloring books on the plane. One good thing was all their suitcases turned up on the luggage carousel. When they walked outside, Allie was waiting in the station wagon for them. Jerry was in the car as well, so they all drove to Lawson Hospital together.

Ten minutes later, they were at the ICU ward asking about Sandy Brown. The nurse on duty said she still wasn't out of surgery. It could be a few more hours before it was done, as it was a very serious operation. They would have to take tendons from her hamstring muscles and skin from her buttocks to fix her arm. Hopefully, they could save it.

"Jerry and Allie, why don't you take Charity down to the cafeteria and see if you can get something to eat. Here's $30. Please bring back a turkey sandwich and some hot coffee for both your grandmother and me. We will be here, waiting for you."

"Okay, Dad. Let's go, Charity, Allie." Jerry put his arm around Charity, smiled wanly at Allie and walked with them to the elevator, pressing down for the cafeteria.

Scott looked anxiously at his mother. "Mom, we need to pray for Sandy. I sense in my spirit that the surgery has hit a plateau. I am worried they might take her arm off."

"Yes Scott, I hear from the Lord Jesus that we need to really intercede for Sandy at this moment. Dear Jesus Christ, you know our desperation. Please, Lord, can you make it possible for them to do a patch job and not cut her arm off at the elbow? May the antibiotics really start working well so the blood infection stops destroying her tissue. I think we need to pray silently in the spirit now, Scott."

"You're right. Let me hold your hand, Mom."

Eventually, Scott's three children came back up to the ward with the sandwiches for their dad and grandmother. While eating the food and drinking the coffee, Scott Brown spotted the lead surgeon coming down the hall to report to them about his wife Sandy's surgery. Allie introduced her father to the surgeon, Dr. Webb.

The doctor took him down the corridor to talk to him privately. "Pastor Brown, here's the good news. The surgery didn't take as long as we thought. It was a ten-hour surgery. The flesh-eating bacteria had destroyed some of the flesh and tendons in her forearm. Because she had been very healthy before this sickness, we were able to take some flesh from her buttocks and tendons from her hamstrings to replace the ones we had to cut out of her arm. At one point we thought she might lose her arm but things started improving and her high temperature and the infection stopped. We can't explain why she is suddenly getting better but we are confident we got all of the dead tissue from her arm. Hopefully she will have a full recovery."

"Thank you, Doctor Webb, for saving Sandy's arm. My mother and I arrived here at the hospital at 4:15 today and we've been praying fervently for the surgery ever since. I think God miraculously stopped the infection and the fever so the surgery could be finished quickly. How long will she need to stay in the hospital?"

While looking intently at Scott, Dr Webb said, "We will have to monitor your wife closely. It will be at least six weeks before she can go home, but only if the infection is completely gone. Once her scars are healed, she will need physical therapy to get the left arm and hand to work again. It will take months to make any headway. Of course, there is her emotional state, too. Whether she will be able to cope with the tragedy of almost losing her arm and being in hospital again, who knows, but we will hope for the best. We have sedated her for now so she doesn't injure her arm once more."

Scott, with tears in his eyes, looked at the doctor, and said, "I'm so grateful you saved my wife's life. It will be hard on us, and especially her, to be an invalid for now. She has always been the tough one in the family, so we will pray she will get through this setback. When can I go and see her?

He replied, "Sandy will be brought back up to the ICU ward in one hour. I recommend only you and your mother go and see Sandy today. She has had a rough go of it and your children could be traumatized to see her in this condition. Normal visiting hours are from 2 to 5 p.m. for ICU and only two people are allowed in at a time."

When Scott told his mother and children what the doctor had said, they agreed Grandmother Brown would take all the children home. She would come back to the hospital at 7 p.m. Hopefully, then the two of them would be able to go in and pray with Sandy.

Two hours later Sandy was back in her private ICU room. Scott saw the nurses working on her and felt sad to see all the tubes and wires hanging from his wife. Just as he was going into the room his mother arrived. They both put on masks and gowns to try and keep Sandy safe from any more infections. The nurse had reminded Scott that Sandy was sedated so she wouldn't bang her arm around. He and his mother stood in the room and quietly prayed. Sandy's eyes were closed but her temperature was normal and she had normal color in her cheeks. They stayed for two hours and left at 9 p.m. Because of this latest tragedy, one of the elders of the church was going to preach the next day.

Chapter 30

Sandy had woken up for a few minutes but her temperature was going up so they had given her more drugs to keep her sedated. Scott was very relieved his mother had agreed to come back to Spokane with him. He didn't know otherwise what he would do with Charity as he still needed to work. Once Sandy was able to leave the hospital, he was planning to take vacation time. She would soon need ongoing physical therapy. He really missed Sandy, and prayed she would come home soon.

Thank God he had sent in his tax return and had just received a $500 refund. That would help with some of the endless medical expenses. Even though Sandy wasn't working right now, her medical office had come up with some sick pay benefits for her. He was also grateful his parents were so generous and his church had medical insurance for his family. Their friend Debra had started a fund through the church to help pay for the medical bills. Apparently, there was already $2000 in the fund.

The children were coping as well as they could, but everyone was glad their grandmother was staying with them. She was a great cook and would always be available to pray if anything was bothering anyone in the family.

Jerry and Allie were enjoying practicing for *Beauty and the Beast*. Every day there was some funny thing that happened at the practice so they could forget about their mother's illness. Josh was doing really well at track and field, winning many competitions and now competing in the long jump, too.

Scott was really missing Sandy and her stable personality in their home. His mother had mentioned he should go back to the counselor,

Kerry Andrews, and discuss the latest tragedy. He was considering it. Because it would be a few months before things were stable again, Scott's father had decided to come back to Spokane as well. Since they had a small townhouse in Seattle, it was easy to leave it for a bit as they had great neighbors who kept an eye on things.

Jerry hadn't seen his mom since her surgery. So, his dad took him up to Sandy's room. It was now two weeks since her latest surgery to fix her arm. Jerry started to tear up when he saw all the tubes sticking out of his mom. They sat there for an hour, feeling helpless and praying she would soon wake up.

Turning to his dad Jerry said, "I never apologized to Mom for how I treated her when I was having trouble with my math class. What if she dies and I never get to say sorry?"

"Jerry, let's pray she doesn't die. You know, I've heard when patients are in a coma, they can still hear you. What if you told your mom how much you regret how you treated her? Maybe if you put your hand on her good arm, she will be able to hear you."

"Okay, Dad, I'll do that. Mom, I just want to tell you how sorry I am for the way I treated you in February. It wasn't right I stonewalled you and wouldn't speak to you. You were just trying to help me. I was wrong to take my frustration at school out on you. Please forgive me. I love you so much, Mom. Please wake up. I'm willing to change. I really miss you."

His dad was crying and patting Jerry on the back. Then he spoke to Sandy. "I'm also sorry about how I treated you. I thought I was in control and had all the answers. Well, God showed me it wasn't true. Please, Sandy come back to us. Lord Jesus, will you give us another chance with Sandy so our family can apologize to her for how we took her for granted? I pray, dear Lord, that Sandy has a chance to forgive us."

They both looked carefully over at Sandy but there was no discernable response. Both of them felt terrible. It really hurt inside to sit there in silence with little hope Sandy would come back to them. For four hours, the two sat in the hospital room at Sandy's bedside watching her. The sympathetic nurse who came and went from the room said there had been no change these past two weeks, and she might never regain consciousness.

Just as they decided it was time to leave for home and get some sleep, Sandy suddenly opened her eyes. She looked directly at Jerry, motioning to him to her bedside. She started whispering something to him. Jerry turned around and looked helplessly at his dad. Scott came beside Sandy on the other side of the bed and put his right ear down near her mouth.

Very faintly he could hear her say, "I forgive you, Jerry. I forgive you, Scott. When can I go home? I want to be with my family and get back to my job. They still need me."

Scott repeated to Jerry what his mother had said. Jerry smiled and hugged his father and ran to tell the nurses. They all rushed into the room and were all smiles at this good development. Everyone asked her how she was feeling.

Sandy whispered, "I don't know. How am I supposed to feel? Why do I have all these tubes in me again?"

"Your husband can tell you what happened with you."

Turning to Sandy, Scott said, "Praise the Lord. God saved your arm. We were hoping he would save it for you. You had a terrible infection so you had to have surgery. Can I give you a kiss, Sandy?"

"Of course, you can kiss me. Where have you been all these days I've been in the hospital?" She beckoned him over and he gave her a careful kiss on her right cheek.

"Oh Sandy, I've missed you. It's been two weeks since you had your surgery and they have kept you sedated so your temperature would go down. I've been coming every day to visit you for three or four hours. My parents have come back to stay at our house while you've been back in the hospital. Thank God they've been looking after Charity as Allie and Jerry have been practicing every day after school getting ready for their musical *Beauty and the Beast*."

Sandy replied, "I hope that I will be well enough to see that musical. I'm really tired now. See you in the morning, right?"

"I love you so much and I'm so happy you're awake, Sandy. See you first thing in the morning," he said as he patted her on her good shoulder.

As Scott and Jerry drove home at eleven p.m., they were very thankful to God. It seemed almost too good to be true. Tomorrow when everyone woke up, they would have to tell the rest of the family the wonderful news.

It had now been three weeks since Sandy had first gone to the hospital and had her surgery. Every day Scott would come by the hospital for two hours to encourage her to work with the physiotherapist. Some days, like today, she would wail and moan in pain when she lifted the weights to try and get her new parts in her arm to work. Scott stood beside her and prayed peace for her. Her tendons would get very sore, and to make matters worse the scar tissue itched every time she moved her left arm. At least her wrist fracture had finally healed. When she got discouraged as she often did Scott would do his best to encourage her by telling silly jokes to get her laughing.

The nurse instructed Sandy to press the button to get more pain medication when she needed it. Sandy didn't want to get addicted to the pain medication but the nurse said it was not addictive. When she finally asked her husband what the problem was with her arm, he told her the truth about the flesh-eating disease. They both cried as Scott held her one healthy hand.

After school that day, he brought all of the children to see their mother for a few minutes. Charity was very sweet, having made her mother a *Toy Story* get-well card. Sandy would always have a smile for Charity and feel better if she saw her, so Scott tried to drive Charity to the hospital every day. They would always have a good cuddle. Every day, Charity made another card for her mother, and asked when she would be coming home, telling Sandy how much she loved her.

Once a week, Allie and Jerry would come by and sing some of their songs from *Beauty and the Beast.* Sandy was hoping she would be home in time to get to see the musical at the beginning of June.

Josh came by right after school twice each week and would tell his mother of all the races he had won that week. He was hoping she would come home soon, too.

Chapter 31

Sandy was on tenterhooks waiting to discover if Scott would finally be able to take her home from the hospital. It had been six long weeks since she had contracted the blood poisoning and flesh-eating disease. She couldn't remember falling or being transported to the hospital. At first, she had been really angry at God when she saw what her left arm looked like now. It was all shriveled, with a huge red scar in the middle of her forearm. And even worse her leg didn't work right anymore because they had taken the tendons from it to put in her arm. It was devastating to her and to Scott that she had trouble walking as well as everything else she was coping with. She was going for physiotherapy for her arm and leg every day for an hour, except on the weekends.

The prayers from her mother-in-law and her friend Debra helped Sandy see the big picture. Debra also arranged for the people from Eagle's Nest Church and Harvest Generational Church to come to the hospital to pray for Sandy for her healing. Her family told her that they were so glad she had survived and not left them to go to heaven. Sometimes when the pain was really bad, she thought it might be better to go to be with the Lord. How was she going to go back to her job when her fingers and arm didn't work right anymore? Maybe there was some kind of voice-activated computer program she could use to put financial records into the computer files. Well, it would take some time before she could even think of going back to her job.

Scott had told her Detective Cassidy was out of hospital and now on desk duty. He could no longer be in the field with his injured shoulder. Rue Smith had seemed to rally but was now unconscious again in hospital. The medical personnel were not sure why she wasn't getting better. The police had found and placed into custody the two men who had beaten

Billy Smith to death. They were currently in jail but their lawyer was trying to get them out on a technicality. They were still waiting to go to trial.

Debra told Sandy that her son, Jake Broadmoor, was worried he would never get a chance to testify against Rue Smith for the damage she did to his former business. Vicki still wouldn't let him come home but she did say hello when he came to pick up the boys for his Saturday afternoon visits.

When Sandy Brown finally left the hospital after two months, she was thrilled. Her husband had bought her red roses, and her mother-in-law Vera had put them in her favorite vase. All the family was there and they had bought pizza to eat at the kitchen table. They made sure she sat at the end of the table and gave her lots of space so no one would bump her bad left arm. Unfortunately, she had not been able to leave the hospital in time to be able to see the *Beauty and the Beast* musical. But it had been tape recorded for her so she was going to listen to that once she had more energy.

Sandy had to keep the arm still covered in a brace unless she was at physical therapy. She was overjoyed to once again be home. Everybody was smiling and telling jokes. Even Charity was telling knock-knock jokes.

Jerry said, "Hey, Charity here's a joke. Why is an orange?"

"Why, Jerry?"

"When it rolls," he said and laughed while everyone else in the family groaned.

Charity replied, "I don't get it. Why's that funny?" Everyone rolled their eyes and her grandfather explained it was just silly and didn't have to make sense.

By seven in the evening, Sandy was already worn out, so Scott helped his wife upstairs to their room. He helped her get changed into her summer pajamas as it was still 70 degrees outside, even in the evening. When she was under the covers, she said goodnight and immediately fell fast asleep.

At eleven p.m., Scott came to bed, relieved to see Sandy was still asleep. At 2 a.m., she woke up screaming. Scott had to calm her down and tell her it was just a nightmare. She was sure that she was being attacked again. He prayed for her and she drifted back to sleep. Scott was so disturbed about Sandy's nightmare that he had trouble getting back to sleep, himself.

Thank God, his father was going to cover for him at the church while Sandy was recovering. Scott was going to take two weeks' vacation. He was so exhausted from all the things that had happened all winter and spring. Not only that, but he was also suffering from guilt for being away when Sandy had collapsed this last time.

Sandy hadn't admitted she was angry at him for being in Seattle when she went back to hospital, but he was sure she was. Tomorrow morning, he wanted to talk to her about this.

The next day, all of the children were at school, and Scott's parents had gone shopping. Scott thought this would be an opportunity to speak to Sandy about everything that had transpired. She was sitting in her favorite spot on the living room couch reading her Bible. Scott came and sat down beside her, being careful not to bump her left arm as he walked by.

"Sandy, I wanted to talk with you about this last incident when you fell ill. I regret I wasn't there when you went to the hospital. It was wrong. What do you think? Could you please forgive me? I know it might take some time for you to be able to do this. How can I make it up to you?"

Sandy looked down at the rug and said, "Scott, I've been disappointed with you about this because it feels like once again you weren't there when I needed you. It's not like you meant to not be there for me but it seems like a pattern to me. My dad was never there when I needed him. My mom would always try to cope when Dad was off on his business trips, but life was chaos without Dad. I remember when you weren't there and I went into labor with Allie. I was so glad your mother turned up and took me to the hospital. I've been thinking it would be good for you to get one of those car phones so I can reach you more easily.

Apparently, they are quite expensive but I think it would be worth it." Looking up, she smiled at him.

Sandy added, "But this time I was the one who told you to go to Seattle for Josh. It wasn't your fault there was a problem with my arm. I didn't know there was a serious problem with my arm that day and thought I could just bear the pain. Jerry was wonderful the way he took charge and made sure I was taken to the hospital. I must thank him and Allie again for saving me. Lewis Lee is a great guy. Thank God he was quick on his feet to help me survive."

"I'm so glad they made sure you went to the hospital that day, Sandy."

"I'm thankful you all prayed for me and I'm still here with you on earth. I remember Jesus Christ talking to me in the hospital, but it seems like a dream. He told me it wasn't my time to go to heaven yet. Unfortunately, he also told me I will have lots of pain but it'll help me to understand the pain and sorrow other people have in life. It will help me to be more empathetic. Jesus also said he would give me a healing gift so I pray that happens. There are some groups here in Spokane like Eagle's Nest Church that have healing services on Friday nights. I am hoping I can go there and learn more about how to pray for other people for healing."

Scott gave her a careful hug on her right side, "How is your pain level, dear? I hope you can manage it."

He added, "Yes, you're right. It's a good idea about the car phone. It would make it easier for you to contact me. Here's some more information for you. My parents have told me they are planning on selling their house in Seattle and moving permanently here to help us with our church."

Sandy smiled at her husband. "Wow, that's great. I know you're not perfect, Scott, but I think the Lord's working on both of our hearts to be kinder to each other and the family. I can see now I have been especially hard on you and Jerry. Would you please forgive me for being so judgmental and critical towards you? Father God is showing me a kinder way. I know through the counselor and scripture that forgiveness is the key. What I would like you to do for me for restitution is to spend these next two weeks with me sitting by my side, reading the Bible to me. I want quality time with you, Scott, where I'm more important than your church work and even the family. I'm not very good at this, but I've decided I need you more than anyone else other than the Lord Jesus."

Scott gave Sandy a hug and said. "My prayers have been answered. I wanted to spend the next two weeks with you, as well. Thank you, God."

Discussion Questions

What caused Sandy to be so angry at Jerry for missing school? In what way was Sandy projecting her pain and anxiety onto Jerry? In Family Systems Theory, the Family Projection Process involves a family member putting a family member like Charity on a pedestal. (Identified Person Positive) or making them the scapegoat like Jerry (Identified Person Negative).

What made Jake vulnerable to being tricked by Rue Smith? What made it so difficult for his wife Vicki to forgive him? In Family Systems Theory, people unwisely become fused to other people during anxious times when they don't have a clear sense of identity. In what way did Jake, Vicki, and Rue either take self or give up self to the other person? In Family Systems Theory, people learn to stand up for themselves and become their true selves through setting healthy boundaries. This is called self-differentiation. How did Sandy help Vicki stand up for herself?

Family Systems Theory talks about emotional cutoff in families as a coping mechanism for reducing anxiety. Emotional cutoff is defined by Dr. Murray Bowen as the process of separation, isolation, withdrawal, running away, or denying the importance of the parental family. How did Jake and Vicki Broadmoor use emotional cutoff to cope with their family crisis? Can emotional cutoff be reversed? Do you see any signs in the book of this happening for the Broadmoor family? Is there any hope for their marriage? Is it possible to forgive an adulterous spouse? If so, how?

Scott and Sandy Brown were concerned about Jerry's wanting to date Samantha. In Family Systems Theory, we observe triangles formed where three people interact, and one is often left out in the cold. What kind of relationship triangles were happening with Scott, Sandy, Jerry and Samantha? You may wish to diagram some family triangles on a piece of paper. You could google the term *genogram* to help you diagram your family triangles. A genogram is a multigenerational map showing the emotional processes in one's family.

When Billy Smith harassed and attacked Sandy's children, how did Sandy and Scott react? Family Systems Theory, as mentioned in our prequel, "For Better, For Worse," talks about the dance of intimacy, balancing closeness and personal space. How can we better balance protecting and valuing the independence of our children?

Did Billy and Rue Smith reap what they sowed? Did it work for them to be in complete control or what they thought was complete control? How did their family of origin affect how they related to other people? In Family Projection Process, people blame others for their problems rather than work on their own selves. Whom did Billy and Rue blame for their difficulties?

How did the Brown family learn to get along better? How did suffering affect them positively or negatively? Have you ever grown through the suffering and difficult times in your life? How has the suffering of Jesus on the cross made you a more loving and forgiving person?

How did prayer make a difference in the Brown family? How does prayer help you in your relationship challenges? Is there any area of your life you need to surrender to Jesus? The term "for" in the word *forgive* means to fully give. How might forgiveness bring a breakthrough for you?

What did you like about Sandy? What did you find painful? How did her anxiety cause her to over-function, becoming over-responsible for her children, particularly Jerry? In your family of origin (immediate family and parents), is there any over-functioning and taking control of others? What helped Sandy to let go and let God?

How would you describe the marital conflict between Sandy and Scott? In what way did their marital conflict help strengthen their marriage? Conflict deepens marital intimacy when differences are embraced and celebrated. How did Sandy's flesh-eating disease help strengthen their marriage and family relationships?

Family Systems Theory talks about strengthening marriage and family through digging for the hidden strengths of one's spouse and family member. How were Sandy and Scott initially at honoring one another's strengths and gifts? How did they improve throughout their family adventures? In your family of origin, did they tend to criticize weaknesses or celebrate strengths as a way of improving others?

When Sandy came out of her coma, what helped her to finally forgive Jerry and Scott? Dr. Gary Chapman, the author of *The Five Languages of Apology*, wrote about the five 'R's of apology:

> 1) I'm sorry (Regret)
> 2) I'm wrong (Responsibility)
> 3) How can I make it up to you (Restitution)
> 4) I'll try not to do that again (Repentance)
> 5) Will you please forgive me? (Request).

Which languages of apology did Jerry and Scott use with Sandy? Which of the five languages of apology did your parents use with you? Which languages of apology do you personally use? Which ones might you be willing to try? You are invited to read Matthew 18:21-35.